THE CRICKET REVOLUTION

THE CRICKET REVOLUTION

Test Cricket in the 1970s

BOB WILLIS
with Patrick Murphy

SIDGWICK & JACKSON
LONDON

First published in Great Britain in 1981
by Sidgwick and Jackson Limited

ISBN 0–283–98759–6
Phototypeset in Linotron 202 Baskerville by
Western Printing Services Ltd, Bristol

Printed in Great Britain by
William Clowes (Beccles) Limited
Beccles and London
for Sidgwick and Jackson Limited
1 Tavistock Chambers, Bloomsbury Way
London WC1A 2SG

CONTENTS

—1—

INTRODUCTION

T H E 1970s were the most influential years the game of cricket has ever known. Never in one decade were so many changes made to the structure of a game that had seemed to defy the passage of time. Before 1970, Test cricket had meandered its way through dull periods – where defensive captaincy had produced stalemates – to exciting, challenging series where the teams seemed to bring the best out of each other. But, whatever the quality of the cricket, its shape, image, and style had remained constant. All that changed in the seventies.

Above all, it became the decade when to win was of paramount importance. Of course, there had been apostles of that creed in great numbers before, but now almost everything became secondary to beating the opposition. Australia, under Ian Chappell, perfected a brand of cricket that involved hard-faced, unyielding attitudes on the field: unnecessary appealing to pressurize the umpires, refusal to walk if the batsman knew he was out, and baiting of batsmen by some of the fielding side. The West Indies eventually twigged the way to play successful modern Test cricket: slow the game down when you are in the field to avoid the rare chance of your speed attack getting collared. The West Indians correctly realized that the fewer balls they delivered per hour, then the less chance there was of being beaten. If the Australians and West Indians were the worst examples of this 'win at all costs' attitude, other countries were not exactly angels. Pakistan brought back their Packer players to prop up their poor side, even though they officially agreed with the International Cricket Conference's hostility towards World Series Cricket. To Pakistan, a Test defeat was a national disaster leading, at best, to the wholesale sacking of the Board of Control, and at worst, to Government intervention.

Nor were England immune from the increase in gamesmanship. Our over rate in Tests had been open to criticism for several years until a fresh system was introduced. Many England players had suffered from bad umpiring on tours, and their attitudes hardened against the principles of sportsmanship engendered in us at school. Tony Greig's

1

influence on the England team in this respect was clear from 1976: we also became a team of non-walkers. It was a logical progression, I suppose, but still one I deplore, because it sums up the essence of the era. When we toured Australia in 1978–9, we appealed more frequently, even though we suspected the batsman might not have been out, as we thought we would get left behind because the Aussies appeared to be intent on appealing for everything, while trusting to the law of averages to favour them. By the end of the decade, you could hardly name a Test batsman who would walk – and that attitude had spread through English county cricket as well.

The decade was dominated at Test level by two sides: Australia and West Indies. England chipped in from time to time, while India, New Zealand and Pakistan occasionally had encouraging victories, though still failing to become major Test sides. Australia dominated world cricket from 1972 to 1976, while West Indies led the way from 1976 to the close of the decade. For both sides, their success was built on one major weapon: speed. Only the very great could master their unrelenting fast bowling for any length of time. Men like Lillee, Roberts, Holding and Thomson were fit and could bowl long spells. They would wear down the batsmen by physical intimidation, the ability to bowl wicket-taking deliveries and the skill to avoid being driven off the front foot. Thus the majority of deliveries from the fast bowlers were 'dot' balls, well-nigh impossible to score off. When the Australians and the West Indians were in the field, the game was less interesting, unless you got your kicks from the sight of great fast bowling. Many people do, but often the sight was less edifying, as batsmen bobbed and weaved at bouncers, unable to lay a bat on the ball.

In 1978, some attempt was made by the Test and County Cricket Board to curb the number of bouncers to one an over, a suggestion rejected by the International Cricket Conference although introduced in English cricket. Yet later that year, the treatment meted out to India's Sunil Gavaskar by Pakistan's Imran Khan and Sarfraz Nawaz showed that Test players would abide by their own rules, unless the umpiring was strict enough.

So the 1970s were the years when a succession of fine batsmen simply became shell-shocked by the relentless battery of fast bowling – men like Amiss, Boycott, Edrich, Kallicharran and Lloyd. They all came again, but only a batsman of that class and experience knows how frightening this all-out pace assault can be. It is true that isolated series like the bodyline one in 1932–3 must have been frightening instances of ordeal by fast, short-pitched bowling, but that has been the fashion for most of the seventies. It almost killed Ewan Chatfield of New Zealand in 1975 when England's Peter Lever felled him with a bouncer, and the same tactic led to India's captain Bishen Bedi conceding a Test in 1976. He closed his second innings at Kingston with five of his team 'absent hurt' because of the punishment dished out by Holding, Daniel, Julien and Holder. But despite the clanging of alarm bells, the game's rulers had done little constructive to curb constant, fast, short-pitched bowling as the decade ended.

My complaints about fast bowling may seem strange, coming from England's main strike bowler of the decade. I have never wanted the game to be anything other than hard and competitive, but I also want it to be fair. I sincerely feel that there is now an imbalance in favour of speed: the fast bowlers are fitter and stronger than ever, many of the wickets world-wide are under-prepared, and much of the umpiring is just not strong enough. I have always felt cricket to be a much more interesting game when the spinners are involved. The most engrossing Tests I have played in were where spin was the connecting factor. The cricket was tight and hard, and the class batsman could still prosper if his technique, footwork, and judgement were sound. At least he did not have to spend all his time wondering if his head was going to be knocked off.

Apart from the Indians' magnificent spinners, the seventies have been lean years for them in Tests. With the retirement of the great Chandrasekhar and the decline of Australia's Jim Higgs, Test cricket entered the eighties without a recognized leg-spinner in its ranks. Slow wickets were partly responsible for this eclipse, but also defensive captaincy – after all, a leg-spinner actually gives runs away as he takes wickets. And there is another problem – he gets through his overs quickly. For many modern Test captains, that would never do.

It is now a common tactic for a fielding side to slow the game down. The public may be cheated of an hour's cricket every day, but a captain does not want the batsmen to have too many balls to hit. So the presence of fast bowlers is even more important, because they take a long time to bowl their overs. And by the end of the decade, we had the ludicrous situation of England facing fines for slow over rates in Tests, while the rest of the countries got away with it scot-free!

The seventies were the years when more money was pumped into the game than ever before and the top players benefited accordingly. After Kerry Packer changed the face of world cricket from 1977 onwards, the

3

cash flow increased, even though sponsorship – in England particularly – had been on the increase before. After Packer, Test players were paid good money for representing their countries – which, after all, was the main bone of contention of Ian Chappell, Tony Greig and the other Packer recruiting agents back in 1977. The game was marketed better, with public-relations men, TV executives and agents all hustling in for a slice of the action. It led, of course, to abuses – particularly Dennis Lillee's behaviour at Perth in 1979, when he held up a Test for ten minutes to get a free, world-wide plug for his aluminium bat. Generally, the game offered a healthy bank balance to the top players by the end of the decade, and in England, young charismatic men like Gower, Gooch and Botham were well on the way to making their fortunes. In English county cricket, the sponsors seemed to be falling over themselves to get into the scene: the John Player League took hold of many fans who could only spare Sundays to watch cricket, the Benson and Hedges Cup (initiated in 1972) led to sell-out crowds at the Lord's final in July, the county championship was sponsored by Schweppes from 1977, and the Gillette Cup remained so popular that the sponsors eventually pulled out of the competition simply because the public associated Gillette too readily with cricket, rather than with razor blades! In addition to all the sponsored competitions, every county was generously supported by local firms on match days, while cash awards for good individual performances by county cricketers seemed to be tumbling out of the trees by the end of the decade.

The great god money had its drawbacks: it led to a trend towards instant cricket that I found gimmicky, yet gave results within a few hours. It brought spectators into grounds, but the style of cricket needed to cope with the runs/overs equation led to diminishing batting standards among England players. Financial considerations also led to more gamesmanship on the field, while I believe umpiring standards slumped throughout the world and became the biggest single problem in Tests. In England, the cash factor meant that from 1974 we played nothing but limited-overs cricket, apart from Tests and the last two innings of a championship match. The popularity of limited-overs cricket was obvious to the game's administrators: television found it a great game to transmit because a result was definite by a certain stage, and sponsors would be delighted to stump up cash if their wares were subtly advertised on TV for millions of viewers. People actually came to watch the one-day brand, while they stayed away from the more specialized three-day version.

4

Inevitably, the popularity of one-day cricket spread to the international scene. On my first tour of Australia in 1970–1, we played our first one-day match against the Aussies. In 1972, the Prudential Cup started in England; in this we play the visiting country three times under limited-over rules. Then the World Cup proved a fabulous success in 1975, leading to doubled receipts for the next one in 1979 and every promise of riches ahead wherever it is staged at four-year intervals. All very satisfying from a financial point of view but, as an unashamed traditionalist who believes that Test cricket is the highest and best standard to be achieved, it worries me that the hold over Test cricket is being loosened by the one-day game. That was brought home to me when I toured Australia in 1979–80; the Australian Board had suddenly fallen in love with one-day cricket, an astonishing turnaround from their attitude in 1970–1, when they did not want it at any price – and indeed their players never could master its skills and disciplines throughout the decade. The Board's change of attitude was due to one thing: money. Test match receipts were down and Kerry Packer had shown them how to market the one-day stuff.

Packer's influence, of course, was crucial on the seventies. His entry into the world of cricket ushered in an escalation of gamesmanship, obsession with money, even greater use of fast bowling, and some ridiculous gimmicks. Packer got a few things right in my opinion, and all the top players have done well out of him, whether or not they joined his W.S.C. The money improved but, just as importantly, he helped to slacken the grip of established cricket on the players. For too long, there had been a master-serf relationship in cricket. Now, with Packer challenging certain established doctrines, the game's administrators had to rethink their attitude. That transition had been easier in England, where the players' union, the Cricketers' Association, had been establishing a working relationship with the T.C.C.B. throughout the decade – indeed the Association played a leading part in mapping out a peace formula between Packer and the Establishment. Packer helped to liberate players from their shackles: for good or ill, men like Barry Wood considered taking the T.C.C.B. to court for a restraint of trade action when he was banned for a time on moving from Lancashire to Derbyshire, and Younis Ahmed took Surrey to an industrial tribunal alleging unfair dismissal. All that was a far cry from the days when I had to kick my heels in Warwickshire's 2nd XI for months in 1972 after leaving Surrey, with never a thought of a chance of redress.

The players became more militant at international level, too. In a

5

curtain-raiser to the Packer Affair, several top Pakistan players had a row with their Board over money on the eve of the 1976–7 tour to Australia. After threats to stay home, the players won major concessions. The Indian stars Gavaskar and Viswanath got into hot water with their Board after taking their wives on the 1979 tour to England, in defiance of official policy. And the England team went so far as to threaten not to play against Pakistan in 1978, when it looked for a time as if the Packer players were being rushed back from Australia to bolster up the Pakistan side.

So the players are more forthright in their views now, and money must bear the brunt of responsibility for that. Money demands that we now play six Test series against the Australians, with a sixth day added on in the last Test if honours are still even. I feel the game is not so enjoyable now, because of money – I find that nobody gives you anything, too many players do not play fairly, and there is an opportunist air about much of Test cricket. We are all on the money-making roller-coaster, and I wonder if we will ever be able to get off it and assess which way our game is going at the top level.

There *are* pluses to cricket in the seventies. Players are much fitter than they were, owing to the extra physical demands of one-day cricket and continuous Test matches. A decade ago, you would never see a side running around the outfield an hour before start of play, and then doing a complex series of stretching exercises. It has led to a greater awareness of the need to work for that extra money; and, in my case, an intensive fitness programme helped make me a better bowler and launched me on a run of thirty-three consecutive appearances in Tests for England, something that would have been unheard of in previous years. Fielding, too, has improved dramatically because of fitness demands: the limited-overs brand of cricket punishes the camels in the field, and the winning teams are the ones with the best fielders to back up tight, accurate bowling. This concentration on fielding has spread throughout the first-class game in the decade, producing some memorable moments: the acrobatics of Randall and Lloyd, the devastating throwing from the deep of Boyce and Walters, the all-round brilliance of Viv Richards and the acrobatic dives behind the stumps of Knott and Marsh. Between 1977 and 1979, England's brilliant fielding allowed us to paper over some cracks, and in several Tests it proved decisive.

Politics entered world cricket in a decisive way in the seventies. South Africa managed to play just four Tests in the first three months of

1970, before the most talented side in its history was put into cold storage for the whole decade. The balance of power on the International Cricket Conference means that there is little chance of re-admission, so many fine South African players will continue to travel the world in search of a comprehensive cricket education. While county cricket prospers, the quality of Test cricket is diluted without the involvement of South Africa, irrespective of the rights and wrongs of the issue. Indeed, the banning of South Africa led to a couple of initiatives that would have taken a lot longer to introduce: the first visit to England of a Rest of the World team in 1970 to play a series that, at the time, was an official Test series, and the World Cup in 1975. On both occasions, South Africa was supposed to be playing Test cricket in England.

Wickets got slower throughout the world as the decade wore on, umpires in England used light meters to try to get teams back on the field, crowds became more unruly, so that players could not walk casually off the field at the end of a Test match day – and in the West Indies and Pakistan there were some frightening riots, fuelled by politics, bad umpiring, and histrionics by the players. In England, the unheard-of happened: a Test was abandoned because the Leeds wicket had been vandalized, and there were streakers and bomb hoaxes at Lord's. After ten years in the England squad, I could not help reflecting on the wise words of my friend and county colleague, David Brown: 'I didn't make a lot of money out of my twenty-six Tests, but the sixties were a much nicer time to play Test cricket.'

After all this time, it still seems remarkable to me that the gawky schoolboy, who religiously watched Test cricket on the television, should end up playing over fifty times for his country. My elder brother, David, appeared to me to have greater natural talent but he pursued an academic career instead of developing his skills as a wicket-keeper/batsman. Luck played a huge part in my early breakthroughs; despite my unorthodox action, I somehow managed to bowl fast, and at a time when England was looking for young, quick bowlers, I simply fitted the bill. When I first played in the Surrey First Team in 1969, I had little idea about fast bowling. I ran up as quickly as possible and simply hurled myself at the batsman; my coach at the Oval, Arthur MacIntyre, tried to get me to bowl in textbook fashion in the nets, but the ball kept going into the side of the net.

John Edrich, noticing how confused I was, took me to one side and muttered: 'Take no notice, just keep going the way that suits you. Don't

7

forget – at least you can bowl fast.' It was Edrich's recommendation that got me on the England tour to Australia in 1970–1. I had just sixty-two wickets to my name in first-class cricket and, although the London press had given me a few rave reviews in the 1970 season, I took no notice of the opinion of some Fleet Street scribes that I should have been initially selected for that tour. Alan Ward's injury meant I was on my way out to Australia in November 1970 – and I know that I have John Edrich to thank.

Since that astonishing experience ten years ago, cricket has taken me to Australia on four other occasions, to the West Indies three times, Pakistan and India once, New Zealand twice, and twice also to South Africa.

The strain of top-class cricket has taken its toll on my physique; two serious knee operations in 1975 and 1981 that almost ended my career, and niggling injuries like pinched nerves in the ribs, sore ankles, and damaged shoulders and feet. As a result, I am now not exactly the sharpest mover in the field and I know my days in the top flight are numbered. At the end of the 1980 season, I felt mentally and physically shattered and one little incident brought home to me just how long I had been in the game. It was at Grace Road, Leicester, and Warwick-shire had won the John Player League in my first year as captain; I was standing triumphantly in the shower and looked around at my companions who were sharing the soap. There were three of them – John Snow, aged thirty-eight, Ken Higgs, forty-three, and David Brown, thirty-eight. None of them was playing county cricket regularly any more and I suddenly thought: 'My God, I played with these blokes years ago! When is it going to be all over for me?'

As yet, I do not know the answer to that, nor do I know what I shall do for the rest of my life. My career is no different from that of any cricketer who has represented his country – a seemingly endless rota of airports, hotel rooms, complaints about overseas practice wickets, innumerable official functions, worried visits to the physiotherapist's table, some riotous drinking occasions, a fluctuating relationship with the media and regular pangs of homesickness. There is never any conception of the passing years until the time for retirement looms; then the memories come flooding back and a feeling of gratitude jostles with a sense of pride that surely nobody would begrudge anyone lucky enough to play professional sport at the top level.

Cricketers with far greater natural talent than me have missed out on the big time and the terrific financial rewards I have picked up in the last few years. I have worked very hard, of course, but without regular bouts of good fortune and consistently sound advice from men like John Edrich, Ray Illingworth, Alec Bedser, Tony Greig, Mike Brearley and David Brown, I would not be looking back on a decade of Test cricket that has seen me take nearly two hundred wickets for England.

2

ENGLAND

ENGLAND'S Test performances over the decade were far from memorable. In my opinion, we had a good side on the 1970–1 tour of Australia, the 1976–7 one to India, and between 1977 and 1979. We were a bad side on two trips to Australia, to the West Indies and to Pakistan and New Zealand in 1977–8. We seemed to go through many transitional periods, without ever getting the right blend of youth and experience: we tried the old guard in 1972 against the Australians and again in the summer of 1976 against the West Indians, and then we went for youth eighteen months later; but the mixture often remained tantalizingly unbalanced. I reckon we only had four consistently great players in the seventies: Boycott, Botham, Knott, and Underwood. That is surely not enough for a country with our tradition and desire to do well at Test level.

Latterly we got the bowling blend right, with Hendrick, Botham, and myself offering variety in seam and swing bowling – even though I have never been able consistently to break through with the new ball early on. Mike Hendrick and I had managed to overcome a terrible run of injuries to achieve full fitness and this gave us a confidence that was boosted by some superb fielding. I have always maintained that our bowling has given us self-respect during the seventies, because our batting has been poor. Now I know I seem biased, and I suppose I do have a down on English batsmen – but I cannot help comparing the guys we had on the 1970–1 tour to Australia with the ones we had nine years later. Men like D'Oliveira, Edrich, Luckhurst and Boycott would sell their wickets dearly: they would give the first hour or so to the bowler, and then make him pay for it later. The modern breed of English batsmen are too flashy. It does not matter how much talent Gower, Gooch, Botham & Co. have; in a Test, you do not get many favours from the bowlers, and you just have to wait for them to get tired or have a loose spell. I think our batsmen sometimes go out and play self-destructively, and show little remorse about it afterwards. If all our younger batsmen followed the example of Geoff Boycott in his attitude

FITNESS

My leg-stretching routines with England physiotherapist Bernard Thomas have delighted picture editors in Fleet Street for years. There is a point to it, though; and Bernard's encouragement and know-how have been invaluable to me in the past, as I have tried to sort out my attitude to fitness. Until 1976 I was a fast bowler who after a time would just run out of steam; but Bernard's help and a series of exercises and a hard running programme got me organized.

Bernard has been England's physio throughout the decade, but he has been more than just a bloke who knows about fitness. He is very well-travelled, shrewd, and approachable: many a young England player has been grateful for some fatherly advice from this friendly man. On tour, he always seemed to know where you could get a bargain to take home; he would know things like the exchange rate, the best places to spend a rest day, and so on – a real Mr Fixit.

to net practice, they would surely be better players. Björn Borg, one of
the greatest-ever tennis players, practises four hours every day, yet
some of our England stars seem to look down on such hard work. They
seem to believe it will all come right in the middle. They lack an
awareness of the good fortune they enjoy – on my first tour to Australia,
I could not get over sharing a room with a guy like Basil D'Oliveira. I
would bring him his breakfast, listen to his words of cricketing wisdom
and drink it all in. If John Edrich told me something on that tour, I
would think: 'Well, that must be right, because he's been playing all
these years.'

Perhaps it is wrong to be so starry-eyed, but I firmly believe that
listening to such experienced men and watching every piece of Test

GEOFF BOYCOTT

This picture sums up the dedication of Geoff Boycott. It is Karachi in 1978, and the rest of the England team are nowhere to be seen. But Boycott carries on batting, loving the feel of the ball on his bat. A great advocate of 'batting for rhythm', he has been an example to our batsmen of the last decade. Others may have been more talented, but Boycott has made everything count when the chips were down. The character he showed when he came back to the side against the Australians in 1977 was admirable: he was on a hiding to nothing from many of our team, who had not forgiven him for choosing when he would play Test cricket again; and the Australians were also gunning for him. But he came out on top – not without a few alarms and controversies in the process – confirming once again that England are more difficult to beat when he is in the side. As he once said to me, 'England want my runs, but they don't want me.' That remark demonstrated the persecution complex he has suffered from, and I could never understand why he took himself so seriously. He possibly got obsessed by being captain of both England and Yorkshire, yet he was strictly a captain by the textbook. He was orthodox and unimaginative, and the only piece of good captaincy advice he gave me was: 'If you think of something, don't put it off – do it.' Judged by his record, he probably did not deserve to keep the Yorkshire captaincy for as long as he did; and when he led England in Pakistan and New Zealand, everything got on top of him.

He is a man with a tremendous cricketing brain, his umpire's reports in New Zealand were astonishing – three foolscap pages, with the time of day that L.B.W.s were turned down, leg-byes not signalled, and everything.

He is not my favourite cricketer by any means, but I have great admiration for many aspects of his career. Cricket has been his life, and he would train hard for his business. Although this has been batting, he has, as a complete professional, made himself into a good, safe fielder. When his mood was right, his contributions to England team talks were tremendously informative. He and Mike Brearley were always a million miles away from each other in ideals: from the time they went on tour with England to South Africa in 1964, Boycott buckled down to the task of becoming a great batsman, while Brearley played for fun and did other things with his life for several years. With that difference in background, they could never get close. Boycott was the better batsman, but Brearley without a doubt the better captain.

DAVID GOWER

Sometimes I get the impression that this side to life in the England team suits David Gower more than the cricket itself. I am sure it is not true, but he seems to give the wrong impression too often. He can be unfortunately glib, even though I know that is just a front for nerves. He *does* worry about his batting, and his role in the team, and he shelters behind a façade of unconcern.

He is the most talented batsman we have had in the seventies – at his best a glorious timer. But when things are not going right for him, he can look amateurish, especially with that wishy-washy stroke outside the off-stump. On his first England tour in Australia, he impressed everybody against the ball pitched well up to him; but the following year, Dennis Lillee and Len Pascoe sorted him out by giving him nothing to drive.

I wonder whether he might have matured if he had been given more responsibility in the England set-up. He might have been on the selection committee on Brearley's second tour to Australia, but Botham got the nod – which served to prolong the meetings, because Ian proceeded to talk all the time, even though he was the junior selector!

A lot of things do not bother David – for example turning up ten minutes late for a team meeting because he has overslept. He is very bright but has a lazy mind; he gets bored with nets, and thinks he can just rely on timing and instinctive skill in a Test innings. Lillee did his best to rid him of that notion.

He is of the young breed of cricketers who has started earning a lot of money out of the game. I just do not know how far he will go. He has got to start batting regularly at number three for Leicestershire, and get some big hundreds under his belt. He must learn when to duck the short-pitched stuff. With his talent, it would be a sin and a shame if he wasted it.

14

cricket I could manage equipped me mentally for the big time. On our 1979–80 tour, some of our young players confessed themselves bored after ten minutes' play in the Test; they wanted to go off and play tennis or walk around the ground, rather than watch and learn from men like Lillee. I was amazed and disappointed. I felt frustrated: I was vice-captain, yet Mike Brearley did not want me or the manager Ken Barrington to interfere with anyone's technique. Players who did not like nets were not made to go in them and work. It may be all very well saying that a bloke selected for his country should be able to sort out what is wrong with his game, but I felt there was a lack of pride in performance, and of application. We had to drop Graham Gooch for the first Test at Perth before he realized what was needed; then he buckled down to net practice, worked out how to play the short stuff, and ended the tour an improved player. Not many others had the same sensible attitude.

David Gower's 98 not out in the Sydney Test was a microcosm of what has happened to our batting. The Press lauded that innings to the skies, but really I thought it was not a good one: there was some tremendous striking at the end, but he could have been out twelve times before he had made fifty. He kept going for his shots, which I think is an admirable attitude in general – but on this occasion he was risky and unconvincing. It was all so airy-fairy and, although that kind of innings stems in part from the demands of limited-overs cricket, nevertheless I feel Gower will have to tighten up his defence if he expects to prosper in Test cricket. He is a player who thrives on instinct and confidence, but I do not believe that a man, however talented, can expect to walk in to bat in a Test without getting a lot of time in the nets under his belt. Gower says that a session in the nets can affect his confidence because the wickets are dodgy, but what is wrong with trying to get the feel of the ball on the bat?

The early seventies saw the last breed of English batsmen prepared to set their stall out and bat for a long time. Men like Amiss, Fletcher, Luckhurst, D'Oliveira, Edrich and Boycott were lucky enough to have learned their trade when there was no need to dash madly for runs because the overs were limited. Like Glenn Turner and Sunil Gavaskar, they built up their defensive technique before extending their repertoire. All of them could score fast if necessary, but they did not believe in giving the bowler much cause for optimism. I feel that in recent years, only David Steele, Clive Radley and Bob Woolmer have shown any of those qualities, apart from Boycott.

15

In common with other countries, our fielding has sharpened up dramatically in recent years. Limited-over cricket means the players have to be fitter, and the England side has been very good in this respect. Tony Greig and Ian Botham have been superb anywhere, Mike Brearley never got the credit he deserved for some fine slip catches, and John Lever has been an excellent outfield, while Graham Barlow, Derek Randall and David Gower have been magnificent fielders thirty yards from the bat. We have been lucky in our wicket-keepers, with Alan Knott and Bob Taylor consistently top class; only Marsh, Kirmani and Bari have remotely approached their standards.

Unlike other Test sides, we have had some good all-rounders, men

IAN BOTHAM

Ian Botham has been a colossus since he came into the England side in 1977. His performances are a statistician's dream; but the style, the aggression, and the confidence stick more in my memory. He took to Test cricket straight away – in his first Test, he had Graham Roope running round for him as twelfth man, doing all sorts of little things for him, and he would freely interrupt the conversations of Test match veterans like Greig, Knott, Underwood and myself. He was the same at the Centenary Test earlier that year: Ian was playing grade cricket over there, yet he attached himself to all the official functions during the Test as if he were one of the twenty-two players.

Not a typically English player, he can hit the ball on the up, and he loves to attack when he plays cricket. Everything has come very easily to him, and he is a terrible example to anyone in the nets, because he gets bored and tries to smash the ball out of sight, instead of playing calmly. All his centuries for England have been dazzling affairs: I particularly remember the one at Leeds against the Indians in 1979. He kept smashing the ball into the crowd, looking up and grinning at me and Brearley, who gave him the 'block it' sign, knowing full well he would take no notice and give us the inevitable rude gesture.

A resourceful bowler, with tremendous variety and that indefinable asset of luck, he will have to take more care of himself in future years if he wants to stay long in the game. When I told him that once, he replied: 'I'm not going to be in this game for very long anyway.' Men like Botham are earning vast sums of money now, and perhaps players of his age are not as hungry to succeed as they were a few years ago. In fact he might even retire if he loses the England captaincy.

When there is no play, Ian gets terribly bored sitting around in the dressing-room. He cannot settle down and read or have a quiet chat; he always has to be doing something boisterous. He never seems to get tired or have any doubts about anything. I honestly think Ian would like to have a friendly punch-up with someone once a week just to relieve his pent-up aggression.

Charismatic, successful and highly talented, he must be well on the way to becoming England's first cricket millionaire. To his credit, Ian does not mind spending his money. Soon he will be losing count of all he is earning – then perhaps the thoughts of retirement might start nagging away at him. He is such a single-minded character that it would be just like him to go out at the top, rather than run the risk of getting kicked on the way down.

JOHN SNOW

John Snow was a really quick bowler when he wanted to be. In Australia on my first tour, he hardly bothered outside Tests; but when he stepped onto the field for England, he could really turn it on. It was a great thrill for me to open the bowling with one of the heroes in my first Test, and the wheel came full circle when I captained him ten years later in the Sunday League with Warwickshire.

Ray Illingworth knew how to handle this sometimes moody, difficult character. He once put his passport on his bed when he stepped out of line in Australia; after that, things were fine. Snow had the typical fast bowler's moodiness, and he was a bit of a loner. He kept a diary on most of his tours, and no doubt included in it some of his clashes with authority. I remember one of our pre-Test dinners in Australia, where collar and tie was the order of the day – but not for Snow. He came in wearing a short-sleeved, open-necked shirt and he was the only one in the room not embarrassed. Then there was the time when he pushed over India's Gavaskar, when he was going for a sharp single off Snow's bowling in 1971. It just had to be at Lord's! In actual fact, I think that incident was blown out of proportion. Snow *did* stop, pick up Gavaskar's bat and lob it to him, rather than throw it at him – but the damage was done, and he was dropped for a Test. He must have been delighted when Packer's offer came along. He was just past his best, but he still had a great reputation out there. When I saw him on the England tour in 1978–9, he told me that he had not stopped travelling all season, but the money was good.

A lithe mover, with a gloriously smooth action, he never took much out of himself, even when bowling fast. Never the favourite son of the powers that be, he should have gone on more England tours and played in a lot more than forty-nine Tests. It would have been interesting to see how he could have retaliated to Lillee and Thomson in 1974–5.

18

like Illingworth and Miller – and we have also had two great ones. Tony Greig and then Ian Botham have been perfect for England's needs: both attacking batsmen, superb fielders anywhere, and bowlers with the happy knack of taking wickets even when bowling badly. When Greig went to W.S.C. in 1977, Botham took over his mantle spectacularly, and he carried the England side for the next two years. I well remember talking to Mike Brearley when we were discussing the England tour party for Australia in 1979–80. He said, 'What the hell do we do if Botham gets injured?' – and that has been a perennial worry to the selectors.

England have struggled in two main departments: batting and fast bowling. We have only had three fast bowlers throughout the decade: John Snow at the start, myself for most of the time, and Graham Dilley at the end. Now I know that speed is not all that essential in England, where the wickets suit the fast-medium seamers more; but it is a serious indictment of our fast bowling potential that we have had so few of them. All over the world, fast bowlers win Tests, and this is one of the reasons why we have had a mediocre time. There is obviously something about the negro body that makes fast bowling an easier job than it is for other races – but if only we had some more English lads willing to work hard at fast bowling, the outlook would be brighter. Fast bowling is very hard work – and it is painful, too, when you are struggling to get fit, or carrying an injury while striving to go flat out. Perhaps hard work is becoming a dirty word in England.

To me, England have made some strange selections for Tests. It is so easy to be wise after the event, but it is frustrating for the vice-captain on tour when he sits in selection meetings for the next Test, sifting the options when he has had little or no choice on the make-up of the touring party. An England tour is always the captain's tour, but I have found it hard on occasions to be dispassionate about some of the players I have toured with. If the vice-captain is to be something other than a figurehead, I think he should be consulted about the tour party. Otherwise you can get a situation where the captain gets injured and his deputy skippers the side in a Test with some players he would not have taken on tour. That happened to me in New Zealand in 1978, when Geoff Boycott had eye trouble and I led the side in the third Test. Our batting line-up was the weakest England one of my career – Boycott, Randall, Radley, Roope, Gatting, Botham, Taylor, Miller, Edmonds, Lever, and myself. Apart from Boycott, only Randall and Botham had scored a Test century (one each), although Radley scored one in that

DEREK RANDALL

Just one of the many run-outs achieved by Derek Randall, the best cover fielder I have known. In this case it was a prized wicket – Sunil Gavaskar at Edgbaston in 1979 – and Derek's infectious delight is obvious.

He is a likeable character, but his humour could wear a little thin after a time when things were going wrong for us. He would chatter away about nothing in particular, and never seem to want the day to end. India took Derek to its heart, and he is a deservedly popular man. His fielding standards have been astonishing: the one feat I shall never forget was the full-length dive to catch Andy Roberts in a one-day international in Australia. There were so many others – the run-out of McCosker at Leeds in 1977, and the one to get Greenidge in the World Cup final of 1979. His speed to the ball, his off-balance throwing, and his anticipation have been remarkable. Unfortunately he spoils it somewhat by some ridiculous appeals for L.B.W.s and catches when he is in no position to judge. That may be just boyish spirits; but he also takes a long time to leave the crease if he disagrees with the umpire's decision.

I never rated Derek's batting at Test level, despite two remarkable

hundreds in Australia: in the Centenary Test, and then at Sydney two years later, when he played a real 'character' knock of 150 to win the fourth Test. He moved around too much and played across the line far too often for my liking. When he was out of form, he would look inconsolable.

A dedicated family man who is very popular, Derek will probably have one of the biggest benefits in English cricket, because of the public affection for him.

The influence of Randall and Gower on England's out-cricket was great. They would each dominate one side of the wicket, so that eventually some batsmen just would not take a single to them, even though there was a long one available. It is a great feeling to have men like these in your side if you are a bowler, because you can afford to put an extra man in a catching position.

I think Randall was more flamboyant and marginally better than Gower in the field, and I once saw a remarkable party piece from him in a benefit match for Mike Brearley. A guy hit a skyer sixty feet up in the air, and Randall got underneath it, put his hands behind his back and caught it!

Test. It was a tour party chosen from the wreckage of Packer; but even then we made the usual mistake of selecting players for Tests who were good in one-day efforts, but not in the real stuff. That has been the theme of many England selections during the last few years – Peter Willey in Australia and Graham Barlow in India were chosen for Tests after doing well in the limited-over game, overlooking the fact that the two brands of cricket are poles apart. We were wrong to ask Derek Randall to open in the Perth Test of 1979 against Lillee, Dymock, and Thomson. His technique – which is not exposed all that much in limited-overs innings – was never up to it.

In my opinion, we should not have sent Fred Titmus to Australia in 1974–5, because of their umpires' views on the L.B.W. law; John Snow should have been in the West Indies in 1973–4 and Australia the following year, because we needed him to answer fire with fire; Bob Woolmer's solidity was missed on the last tour of Australia. David Steele should have gone to India under Tony Greig, but Greigy and Alan Knott had bees in their bonnets about Steele's inability to play the spinners. They remembered Barry Wood's traumas of the previous tour, and assumed another opening batsman in the same mould might suffer a similar fate. I believe Steele was cast aside far too soon after standing up bravely and successfully to a fearsome array of Australian and West Indian fast bowlers. His defensive forward prod would have suited Greig's passive policy against the Indian spinners. I think Mike Brearley was unlucky to be dropped in the 1976 series against the West Indies after some skilfully defensive batting at Lord's. Brian Close and David Steele alternated as makeshift openers, and that robbed the middle order of solidity.

Steele could easily have been picked for England before 1975: he had been around for a few years, making runs in county cricket in a no-nonsense fashion. Alan Jones of Glamorgan might have had a chance to establish himself – he played one game against the Rest of the World in 1970 and Procter got him cheaply twice, a fate that befalls many high-class batsmen. He was dropped after just one match and never got another chance, even though he has scored thousands of runs year after year. Ray Illingworth did not rate his fielding ability all that highly, but surely Jones deserved an opportunity to prove that he could bridge the great divide between county and Test cricket?

Dennis Amiss was in and out of the England side until he consolidated his position in 1973. He never really got the chance to settle down in those early days: he always felt he was on trial, and so he never did

DEREK UNDERWOOD

Derek Underwood was, in my opinion, England's greatest post-war bowler. Covered wickets in Tests may have reduced his effectiveness in recent years, but he could still destroy a side if the wicket helped him, or keep things quiet if necessary.

A philosophical character who never wanted the responsibilities of captaincy, he was never any trouble to the Establishment until he signed for Packer. Before that he was simply 'Dapper Deadly', the smart dresser with the short hair and the happy family background. He was always insecure: he had been dropped by England several times, and never assumed he was an automatic selection.

Unathletic, a regular smoker who liked his beer, he never took to all this training lark. He was an old-fashioned cricketer who apparently could not get used to the new group of England players who simply were not on his wavelength. Very loyal to his friends and his family, Derek seemed unhappy during his spell with World Series Cricket: he missed identifying himself with a national team, plus his nights out and a few beers with his old team-mates.

He liked to bowl for about ten minutes in the nets, just to check that everything was in working order. He would help the lads out in the nets for longer than that, but he did not like it. He worried that he would start experimenting and lose his rhythm. For such a talented bowler, Derek worried far too much.

ALAN KNOTT

I think Alan Knott was the greatest wicket-keeper of my time, and – considering his consistency – surely one of the best of all time. His batting all over the world for England was resourceful, audacious, and reliable. Geoff Boycott has good cause to thank Knott for helping to revive his Test career when he was struggling in his Trent Bridge comeback against the Australians – before Knott walked to the wicket, Boycott could hardly get the ball off the square. Knott galvanized him with his amazing cheek and nerve in taking on the Aussies and making Thomson and the others look less lethal than Boycott had done previously. The rest is history.

I was not surprised that Knott signed for Packer: he was never a happy tourist when his wife was not there, and he was delighted with the chance of security and family stability with World Series Cricket. Apart from that, he was a great disciple of the gospel according to Greig. I remember Knott telling me after one tour of the West Indies that Greig would win a Test in Australia the following winter with his off-breaks. I thought that a little fanciful at the time, and Greig never made real advances as a spinner.

A meticulous man, Knott would sort out his own laundry, and in the morning his bathroom routine would take ages. He always wanted to wear his own pads, even in W.S.C. He did not like straps round his pads, so he would use white tape to make him feel more comfortable. He thought the buttons round his cuffs were too tight, so he would tape the cuffs. All the time in Tests, his lucky hankie would stick out of his flannels, and his lucky teddy bear would be in his bag.

He was fanatical about food and uncomfortable to eat with, because he went through the routine of polishing all the cutlery and asking for certain types of food. He kept in regular contact with our physio, Bernard Thomas, at all hours on tours.

A worrier and a pessimist, he thought he would stiffen up later in his career – which is why he did all those limbering-up exercises. But, personal foibles apart, he was a great Test match performer with a wonderful temperament. He grew in stature for the big occasion.

---

himself justice. I thought Keith Fletcher was discarded too soon; he was shaken up by Lillee and Thomson, but so were most good players, and that was before the helmets were donned. Despite some unconvincing performances, Fletcher had a very good Test record, and there's no doubt in my mind that he would have been a better proposition in later years than some of the younger brigade.

This policy of chopping and changing led to insecurity among many England players. Derek Underwood was a prime example: it used to

amaze me that he often expected to be dropped. He was passed over in favour of Norman Gifford on a few occasions, and Underwood never forgot that. He thought that one bad Test would be the end of him – an astonishing attitude, considering his gifts and achievements.

England have never really sorted out their attitude to a second wicket-keeper on overseas tours. Roger Tolchard was a good choice as understudy to Alan Knott on the Indian trip, because he could bat at number six and field very well – and so it proved, with him helping

MIKE BREARLEY

Mike Brearley played a decisive role in keeping the England side together after Kerry Packer entered the stage. Mike was a big fan of Tony Greig, and seemed far from an opponent of World Series Cricket – and he saw no reason why the English Packer players should drop out of the side when the Australian ones would be up against us in the 1977 series. I think he was right, and the atmosphere in the England dressing-room remained a harmonious one under his leadership until his second tour of Australia, where he seemed preoccupied with personal problems and unreasonably dogmatic about some aspects of the preparations for the Tests.

Tactically, Mike was a very sound captain, knowing when to turn the screw, when to con a batsman with an unusual field setting, and how to get the best out of his bowlers. He did not like Australia – I can't think of anyone further removed from the brash Aussie image – but his captaincy on his first tour out there was a model to anyone wishing to learn the game. He outclassed poor Graham Yallop at almost every turn. He shares the fault of many cricketers of taking an all-or-nothing view of a player: if he saw someone play very well one day, he would convince himself that he was a good player most of the time. I remember his enthusiasm for Derbyshire's Kim Barnett, who bowled leg-spinners at us in the nets in Australia. Mike asked: 'Why isn't this bloke out here on tour with us?' It had not occurred to him that our batsmen were not good enough to play Barnett properly. He also seemed to develop a bit of a blind spot about John Lever: time after time, John would be named twelfth man, or given a bowl as a last resort, and his confidence got very low as a result.

Mike once admitted to me he was a little tight with his money and certainly he drove a hard bargain on commercial matters. But unlike Tony Greig, who was motivated by materialism, Mike wanted money to help establish himself in the psychoanalysis career he is determined to enter when he finishes with cricket. It remains to be seen how long cricket can hold him: certainly he is the brightest man I have met, too bright perhaps to enjoy the earthy atmosphere of the players' bar. Mike was not a great one for hearty camaraderie, although he did a great job in knitting together all the different temperaments in the England side. There was one exception: Phil Edmonds, himself an intelligent, articulate, opinionated man who used to infuriate Mike. Their set-tos usually made amusing listening.

Tony Greig in a partnership that won the Calcutta Test. It seemed as if the idea of a utility man who could keep wicket had been accepted – yet Paul Downton went as understudy to Bob Taylor the following year on the Pakistan and New Zealand tour. He hardly got a game – Taylor's performances were consistently brilliant, and we could have done with another batsman. The same fate had befallen Bob Taylor on previous tours, when Knott's consistency kept him out. All I thought was needed was to pay a reserve keeper to remain fit back home and take a batsman who could keep adequately. Despite the weakness of the England batting, we are still pursuing the traditional policy.

No subject has fascinated cricket writers in the seventies more than that of the England captaincy. There seems to be a period of honeymoon, when the new skipper enjoys a harmonious working relationship with the Press; but then they eventually turn on him. Mike Brearley experienced that: an instant success with the media in 1977, he was genuinely hurt when so many disparaging things were written about his batting in the following year. He was too balanced an individual to allow it to eat into his soul, but it only increased the pressure on him. The England side ached for him to succeed with the bat, and our relief when he got fifty against the New Zealanders at Trent Bridge in 1978 was great indeed. Ironically enough, Mike Brearley reverted to his best form when he handed over the England captaincy, and could well have been recalled to the team as a batsman on merit.

27

RAY ILLINGWORTH

Even in his last year as England captain at the age of forty-one, Ray Illingworth was still good enough to beat a player as fine as Roy Fredericks in the air, and present Alan Knott with a stumping chance. Illy did not bowl too much because of back trouble in his later years, but he could still turn it on.

He was my first England captain and, even though I would have played cricket for England under the captaincy of John Cleese if necessary, I was still very impressed with him. He was always in charge, everything emanated from him: the players had the feeling that all they had to do was turn up at the ground and leave the rest to Illy, he would take care of everything. He liked a drink, but he always seemed in control of his faculties. A very shrewd man, he knew how to turn things to the advantage of himself and his team. The loyalty of his players was insisted upon, and nobody stepped out of line for long with Illy: he sorted out John Snow on the Australian tour when he seemed to be going through the motions at times. He did the same to Geoff Boycott at Lord's in 1973, after Boycott had got out near the end of the day and blamed it on Brian Luckhurst for not keeping the strike. Illy cracked down on Boycott very sharply.

He had a Yorkshireman's chip on his shoulder about being on so many tours with amateurs who got extra privileges. He wanted things to be levelled off among all the tourists, and he would fight like hell for his players. His relationship with the Establishment was always uneasy after the Australian tour, and we had the suspicion that the knives were often out for him. When he turned down the Indian tour of 1972–3, that was another nail in his coffin. A less democratic leader than Brearley, he had the same knack of making you want to play for him.

The only England captain in my time whose form was not undermined by the captaincy was Ray Illingworth. Mike Denness, Tony Lewis and Mike Brearley were all short of Test class at the time, while Tony Greig had a bad time with the bat and ball against the West Indies in 1976. Illingworth was worth his place in the side as a player, quite apart from his superb captaincy. Few modern captains have had such a difficult series as Illy in 1970 against the Rest of the World; Guinness' sponsorship alone ensured the World XI would try their hardest for the generous prize money, and their galaxy of talent won the series 4–1. Yet England were not disgraced and the margin could have been closer; through it all, Illingworth's all-round skills were an inspiration, and it was the same story in Australia.

I think the biggest mistake Illy made was in not going on the tour to

India in 1972–3. He wanted a rest, so they sent out Tony Lewis instead, even though his batting record in the 1972 season was poor. He was a popular captain, and the heat was on Illy when he took over the captaincy again for the home series against New Zealand. In the side was Tony Lewis, which was ridiculous considering his indifferent form. Lewis lasted just one Test after getting four runs in two innings and although Illy had beaten off one challenger, his time was nearly up. After a thrashing later that summer from the West Indies, he was sacked in favour of Mike Denness for the West Indies tour. It was surely unfair to ask Denness to captain the side for the first time on such a difficult tour. I reckon Illy should have gone as captain, with Denness as his deputy to learn the ropes. In the following year there were no challengers to Denness for the Australia tour, even though his batting record for the 1974 season was not much better than Mike Brearley's four years later, when many were saying Brearley was not worth his place in the side. But in 1974 Boycott had dropped out, and Tony Greig had burned his boats for a time following the controversial run-out of Alvin Kallicharran at Port of Spain. Donald Carr was manager on that West Indies trip, and the secretary of the T.C.C.B. had taken a very dim view of that incident. So Denness went as captain to Australia on a terribly arduous tour for him, and all he really did was keep the seat warm for Greig.

I think the Establishment always felt a little uneasy with Greigy: his flamboyance and eye for money weren't among the usual credentials for the post. He faced a difficult time at the beginning against Lillee and Thomson and, all things considered, I thought he did a fair job. He definitely helped build up a good team spirit, and when Mike Brearley took over in 1977 it was a harmonious, settled side that greeted him. Such a side is often a successful one, no matter what the Press and those who want to get into the team may think. Security breeds confidence, which in turn leads to talented players doing themselves justice – and some of our selections over the years have not inspired confidence.

Alec Bedser has taken most of the flak as chairman of the selectors. I think Alec has been a misunderstood man over the years: just because he doesn't get carried away by young, attractive-looking players, the Press think he is a bit of a stick-in-the-mud, and that he is stunting the development of talented players. It is true that Alec looks at the vast sums of money we make, and compares things with when he was a player; but that does not warp his judgement of what constitutes a Test cricketer. Nobody can tell Alec Bedser anything about that: as a player, his record was superb, and I respect his honesty and values. Many young players may find it boring to hear Alec going on about the need to practise in the nets, but I believe he is absolutely right. If some of us put half the work into our cricket that Alec does into his job as chairman of the selectors, we would be better cricketers. He has done a hell of a lot for England in the seventies, even if he has been out of tune with many of the things that have become fashionable in cricket.

I have no idea how long Alec will stay in the job. Even his huge reserves of patriotism and optimism risk being worn away, and I hope he does not wear himself down by the sheer slog of his task. It cannot be much fun at his age, rushing up and down England to see batsmen who do not know how to build an innings and bowlers who waste the conditions, and then opening a newspaper to see some cricket writer

ENGLAND STOPS WALKING

England toughened up towards the end of the seventies; and one man directly responsible for that was Tony Greig. This picture aptly summarizes Greigy's attitude to walking. At Old Trafford in 1977, the TV playback showed that the ball from Australia's Jeff Thomson had deviated off Greigy's glove, but he got away with it. The Australians could not believe it. When Greig reached his fifty, Rod Marsh made a point of clapping his hands sarcastically above his head. The irony of the incident was that the Australians had been the apostles of non-walking for as long as anyone could remember. By the end of the decade, the batsmen I knew who would walk could be counted on the fingers of one hand.

31

BOYCOTT'S COMEBACK

Triumph and despair for Geoff Boycott in 1977. After an exile of three years he got back in the side for the Trent Bridge Test against the Australians, and proceeded to run out the local hero, Derek Randall. The pressure on him was immense: the Aussies had their own theories about why he had been missing from the Test scene for three years, and they really put him through the mangle. But he survived and he scored a hundred and an unbeaten eighty on his comeback.

A fortnight later, Boycott was the nation's hero at Leeds. He had just completed his hundredth hundred, and at close of play the demands of television forced him to rush through the back-slappers among his home crowd. It seemed a long time since he last played for his country – at Old Trafford in 1974.

telling a man who took 236 Test wickets how he should run a Test team. He has made mistakes, of course; but if ever a man deserves a better decade for England, it is Alec Bedser.

3

KERRY PACKER

UNTIL May 1977 the name of Kerry Packer was known only to the media in Australia and to those who watched his Channel 9 entertainment from Sydney. Thereafter, he became as famous as any cricketer – because he staked his professional reputation on improving the financial lot of many of the world's best players. He signed up the captains of England, Australia, West Indies and Pakistan in a cloak-and-dagger operation that took the game's ruling bodies completely by surprise. Test cricket suddenly had a rival because Packer's huge wealth and grandiose ideas had tempted away so many great players. The world of big business entered top-class cricket in 1977 because of Packer's intervention – and the shape of the game changed for evermore.

There is no doubt in my mind that his influence has cheapened Test cricket. Time will tell whether it recaptures its hold on the public; but after Packer's entry into world cricket, we have had several years of sub-standard play at the highest level. This was partly due to the fact that most of the sides lost many of their finest players – so that, until 1979, certain cricketers were picking up vast sums of money that were out of all proportion to their abilities. The desire for money shared by both players and administrators meant too much Test cricket was being played throughout the world. Television had woken up to the fact that cricket was a relatively cheap game to broadcast and that, provided the play was sufficiently entertaining, it was a 'good product'. The administrators of cricket also wanted extra Tests to be played because it meant more cash for the respective Boards of Control. The one-day internationals became important because that seemed to be the kind of instant, gimmicky brand of cricket that more and more people preferred. We still played a lot of Test cricket as well, so that eventually there was an air of familiarity about it all. It is not good for the mystique of Test cricket to have the England team in Australia two years in a row; you can have too much of a good thing. The same applies to the West Indies in England: they toured England four times in six years after 1975.

Many harsh words have been spoken about Packer and there have been faults in abundance on both sides. As a confirmed anti-Packer man myself, it is only fair that I should acknowledge his pluses. The camera work on Channel 9 was superb, and night cricket was terrific entertainment and a great idea, while the marketing techniques of W.S.C. were a real eye-opener. When night cricket came to Sydney, huge crowds flocked to see it for the first time; the turnstiles were jammed with people trying to get through, and thousands were still outside when the game began. Packer went out and told the gatemen to save time and let the rest in for nothing. That is good public relations: people love something for nothing. He provided free parking and free transport to many of the grounds, and he realized that there was an untapped reservoir of support from those who wanted to watch cricket at night after they had finished work. He was aware that Australia is a sports-mad nation, and that if he made the game less specialized and more Americanized, with a strong emphasis on the personality cult, then he had a chance of success. W.S.C. was wound up before one could properly assess its chances of long-term success, but not before it gave a lesson to the Establishment in how to promote itself. W.S.C.'s public-relations sense was very good: all those coaching clinics run by world-class players were terrific for any cricket fan, and Eddie Barlow and others did a great job in the country districts, playing on poor-quality wickets but spreading the gospel and signing autographs till all hours. I am sure the improved showing of W.S.C. at the turnstiles in its second year had a lot to do with the pioneering work done in the country games.

Kerry Packer also helped those who stayed within Test cricket. In 1977, Test fees for English players went up from £250 to £1,000. True, they were due to go up to £500 anyway, and the T.C.C.B. had been looking at the prospects of sponsoring Test fees for eighteen months before Cornhill Insurance came to the rescue – but there is no doubt that the threat of defections to W.S.C. led to an acceleration. What is not true is the oft-repeated theory that W.S.C. helped the average county cricketer get better wages. Tony Greig gave this as one of the main reasons for signing for Kerry Packer, but I remain as sceptical of his reasoning as I was then. The minimum-wage structure for English county cricket was already well advanced by the time Kerry Packer appeared. It was carried through sensibly by the T.C.C.B. and our players' union, the Cricketers' Association. I believe it is unfair for Packer to claim credit for that, because I do not think he has benefited

35

MOONLIGHT CRICKET

Cricket by moonlight at V.F.L. Park, Melbourne, in the second season of World Series Cricket. Although we traditionalists were sceptical about many aspects of W.S.C., there is no doubt that night cricket was a great idea. Even if few people turn up, there is always a better atmosphere than in the daytime – I feel the same about soccer matches. The crowd gets more involved, and the whole thing seems more vibrant. It is ideally suited to the Australian philosophy of giving the public what they want: many were getting disenchanted with the daytime variety; and night cricket was a good excuse to down a few cans of beer, look at the women, have a brawl if the fancy took you, or enjoy seeing the ball hit regularly into the crowd.

The English climate isn't exactly ideal for night cricket, but there is no reason why it can't occasionally be an entertaining money-spinner, provided that it is properly marketed and costed.

any English players, apart from the élite who manage to play Test cricket. The vast majority of bread-and-butter cricketers owe at least one-third of their salaries to Test Match receipts – and that was an area which W.S.C. was trying to undermine.

Although W.S.C. helped act as a catalyst and made the games administrators think more deeply about ways to sell cricket to the public, nevertheless it had a harmful effect in many areas. Double standards were rife in the cricket world during the years of W.S.C. – in England, counties such as Kent and Somerset refused to take a stand against their Packer players, even though they were undermining the financial structure of the English game by associating with a brand of cricket that was in direct opposition to Tests. Warwickshire seemed the most consistent county during that period: our committee felt that Dennis Amiss should not have his cake and eat it, so he could either play for W.S.C. or Warwickshire, but not both. That view was supported by the majority of our players, and those were unhappy times in our dressing-room. Hardly a word would be spoken to Dennis during the day, and he would sit writing letters on W.S.C. note-paper. I felt that Dennis should never have played again for Warwickshire after he signed, and our relationship sadly deteriorated. The situation was further polarized at Edgbaston because Warwickshire has such a strong connection with the Establishment. Our club has several officials serving on influential committees at Lord's; our secretary, Alan Smith, has been a Test selector; I had captained England by that time; and David Brown, our former skipper at Warwickshire, was the chairman of the Cricketers' Association.

They were strained times at Edgbaston and I am glad it blew over – but at least we stuck to our guns, unlike other counties.

Some countries took strange decisions over Packer. Australia's Board of Control was predictably anti-Packer in 1977, yet when Bobby Simpson took his young side to the West Indies, there were no complaints that they were facing up to the W.S.C. West Indians. Also in 1978, Pakistan dithered about playing their Packer men. The England players threatened to pull out of a Test if they were selected, but that only delayed the inevitable and, a few months later, they were back in the fold, facing the arch-enemy India. After all, the Pakistanis wanted to win, so the support given by their Board to the I.C.C.'s abortive attempt to ban Packer players from Test cricket faded into insignificance.

But the biggest volte-face was that of the Australian Board once they

37

TONY GREIG

This shows the two sides of Tony Greig: in the first picture, he is chaired off the field at Madras in 1977, after his inspiring captaincy had set England on a course that eventually gave them the series 3–1. This was Greig's finest hour as captain – yet within weeks, he was taking a deliberate step that he must have known would lose him the England captaincy and lead him to becoming a TV pundit on Kerry Packer's Channel 9, interviewing such men as his close friend and successor as England captain, Mike Brearley. Greigy suited the world of TV: a money-conscious extrovert, he was a great marketing man for whichever brand of cricket he was pushing at the time. His role as Packer's agent was rewarded by the promise of a top job for the rest of his life; and, in the affluence of Sydney, that will probably be good enough for Greigy. Tony really enjoyed being interviewed when he was captain; men like Brearley and Illingworth would do it very well and willingly as part of the job, but they could take it or leave it. Greigy positively basked in the limelight. Articulate, charming, and frank, he was a natural.

As a cricketer, he was modest at county level and tremendous in Tests. No cricketer of my time has varied so much in his performances at Test and county level. He was a big occasion player par excellence – combative, resilient, with the guts to play his shots and buy his wickets, and one of the best all-round fielders England ever had. He had been brought up in South Africa, and he brought all their gifts of commitment and aggression to bear in Tests. Perfect as a Test all-rounder, he could not sustain it in county cricket, because the spark of atmosphere was missing. As a bowler he did not use his height enough to make the ball bounce awkwardly; but he could seam it around, and he took good wickets all round the world. Many said he was a lucky bowler, but so is Ian Botham, and they had one thing in common: they bowled for wickets. Mike Hendrick has been technically a far better seam bowler than Tony Greig, but whose record is better in Tests?

I didn't know he suffered from epilepsy till he had finished in cricket. I do remember that he always insisted on sleeping in our dressing-room at some stage of the day, and I thought that strange at the time. Once I went into his room to wake him when we were on tour in India. He took a long time to wake up and he was clearly under the influence of some mild drug. He did tremendously well to conceal it from us, and that only increased my admiration for what he achieved at Test level.

I first played under him at Leeds in 1976 and I was enormously impressed by the way he geed me up. He seemed to understand that a fast bowler needs a boost to his ego, and he kept telling me how important I was to England, and so on. That was shrewd psychology, because I needed encouragement after a nightmare series of injuries; and I went from strength to strength under his captaincy. He was still

geeing me up in the 1977 series against Australia, even though he was no longer captain.

I think history will prove him to be a much-maligned man. I do not blame him for keeping the Packer thing a secret: in any business deal you don't show your hand till it suits you, and perhaps it is too easy to romanticize on behalf of the Establishment. Greigy was the current England captain, but there was no justification for believing that he would remain so for several years. Once his smooth-talking skills were won over by Packer, it was in the bag. Greigy could charm the birds from the trees if he wanted and he was an ideal agent.

Although I liked him and admired him for lots of things, our basic philosophy was different. I am a patriotic Englishman who isn't totally motivated by money, while Greigy has lived in three continents and is unashamedly materialistic. Anyway, I wish him well.

39

had made their peace with Packer. After having castigated him as the devil incarnate for the previous two years, they did a deal with Channel 9 that involved the players of Australia, the West Indies, and England fulfilling a murderous itinerary of six Tests and endless one-day internationals in 1979–80. The Board's motivation for this was one thing: money. They had lost money for the first time, and in the process diluted the appeal of Test cricket.

I never met Kerry Packer, and the fact that he has had some harsh words to say about me on television is neither here nor there. I could never work out why he didn't accept that the Australian Board was tied to the A.B.C. network for televising Tests until 1979 – after that, there was every justification for thinking that Packer's money would get what he wanted, once the contract for exclusive TV rights was put out to tender. What Packer tried to get in 1976 he ended up with in 1979 – but at great financial cost to himself and to the world of cricket. Presumably the money was a drop in the ocean to him, but was it that much of a blow to his ego that he was told to wait till A.B.C.'s contract was up?

I shall never know why he did not sign up an entire English squad of players. They need not have been the best ones around: any English side would have been ideal, because the Aussies would have thrashed them out of sight and the crowds would have flocked in to see the Poms hammered. As it was, the World XI and the West Indies team were far too strong for an Australian side that had looked distinctly weak in England in 1977. The massive home crowds that watched the annihilation of England and the West Indies proved that the Aussies will turn up in droves to watch their blokes winning – but if the boot is on the other foot, they will stay away. England's only representatives in W.S.C. were three players who were not suited to its style or were simply past their best (Woolmer, Snow, and Amiss), two world-class players (Knott and Underwood) and their captain, Tony Greig, who simply fell apart in cricketing terms. I think a complete England XI would have been a winner.

This lack of national identity was one of the things that put me off W.S.C. When I was offered 25,000 dollars a year for five years by Richie Benaud and Tony Greig during the Oval Test in 1977, I told them I was interested but could not work up much enthusiasm for the idea of playing for a World XI. I did not believe there was all that much comradeship between Test-playing countries, for the game had got more ruthless as time progressed; and I told them so. Tony Greig told me that the cash would be the great motivation for me – and in that answer he hit on the differences in our attitude. I could not play cricket purely for money; I need the good fellowship of county cricket, and the comradeship you get from touring with men you have known for years. I wanted to play for my country, not a World XI. I also knew that signing for Packer would mean the end of my career at Warwickshire, and I definitely did not want that. They had been magnificent to me during those seasons when I was invariably out of action with injuries, and I wanted to repay their kindness and loyalty in some way.

I have done very well out of turning down Packer. I became a favoured son in the eyes of the Establishment, and I was a regular vice-captain of England on tours abroad afterwards. Money started flowing in from all sides after 1977, and a lot of that must stem from Packer's catalyst. It was a far cry from the days when I was on the dole in an English winter. I did not blame my colleagues in the England team for signing, although I believe that Derek Underwood might have stayed in the Establishment fold if he had known that Cornhill's sponsorship was on the way. I think Alan Knott would have signed anyway, because he was fed up of touring without his wife; and for Dennis Amiss and John Snow it must have seemed like Christmas as they approached the end of their England careers. Tony Greig was attracted by the money and the glory, plus the fact that he genuinely admired Packer and loved Australia, while I am sure that Bob Woolmer was spurred on by his ego. He liked the idea of being recognized as one of the world's top fifty players – even though his style of batting was totally foreign to Packer's razzmatazz – and he was a long way from a benefit at Kent.

They all had good reasons for joining, and good luck to them, but I do think they got a bit one-eyed – they kept saying 'Kerry's doing this' and 'Kerry's doing that', so that it was like listening to a propaganda machine. I suppose we anti-Packer players became equally dogmatic: once you take your stand, I think subconsciously you do your best to denigrate the other side. Certainly men like Bob Taylor, Geoff Boycott, Mike Hendrick and John Lever were as entrenched as I was in anti-Packer attitudes, and we lost no chance in deriding the fancy coloured clothing and all the gimmicks when we first saw W.S.C. on TV. Our minds were closed at that time, because we were carrying the banner for Establishment cricket and trying to fight back. Our management asked us not to go out of our way to see the W.S.C. players because the Press would make a big thing about it. Tony Greig asked us all to his house when we stayed in Sydney, and some of our lads went up to see a

DENNIS LILLEE

This picture sums up the Dennis Lillee of the late seventies. He became the most famous figure in Australia, and I think he loved the glamour of it all. Dennis seemed to get obsessed with money; he decided to put on a show for the public, provided that he was well paid in return. He was – and the Australians loved him for his wild excesses, his baiting of the umpires, his ridiculous appeals, and his superb bowling.

Can you imagine an Englishman getting away with that aluminium bat nonsense at Lord's? Holding up the game for ten minutes so that he could plug his wares, and berating Mike Brearley for his perfectly reasonable objections? Lillee seemed to get more and more incensed on the field – or perhaps he was just a great actor.

He was certainly a great fast bowler, the best I have seen and one of the finest of all time. He had everything: courage, variety, high morale, arrogance, supreme fitness, and aggression. We both started our Test careers in the same series – 1970–1 – and I wish I had had his gifts. I admire the way he came back after a bad back injury, working himself to exhaustion for a year till he was ready. Years after that injury, it still gives him some pain.

He was a wonderful sight as a bowler; but I am afraid I will also remember him as the bloke who stopped playing for love of the game and his country, and started playing for money and to please the TV producers.

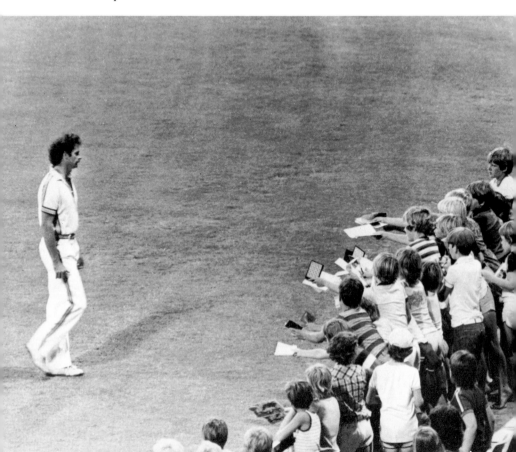

bloke we all liked. I did not go, not out of any deep motives, but simply because I knew Greigy would monopolize the conversation with talk about himself and W.S.C., and I could not take much more of all that.

Cricket was the real loser in that 1978–9 season in Australia. There was just too much of it – we were rushing around, playing six Tests and one-day internationals as well as doing a lot of promotional work on behalf of 'fair dinkum cricket' while W.S.C. was churning out its product as remorselessly as the hamburgers extolled incessantly on Channel 9. Something had to give, because neither side was exactly prospering.

It was with some relief that a truce was negotiated in April 1979, because the sack was still hovering over Dennis Amiss at Warwick-shire, and there were many rumblings among the England players about the West Indies bringing their Packer men over for the World Cup in two months' time. But W.S.C. kept its cards close to its chest about winding the whole thing up: at the April meeting of the Crick-eters' Association, Alan Knott stood up and gave us a great long speech about how marvellous it was to serve two masters, and what great things had happened to cricket since Packer, and so on. David Brown, the Association chairman, was amazed that Knott did not know that a settlement was in the wind.

I think the Association came out very well from the Packer Affair. At times, the Establishment and Packer broke off negotiations in a fit of temper, but it was the Association – in the persons of John Arlott, David Brown and Jack Bannister – that kept both doors slightly ajar. I know I was impatient with them on occasions, because I wanted some of the more extreme proposals voted on at the special Association meetings; but their wise counsel won the day. Certainly Dennis Amiss has reason to be grateful to the Association's executive for smoothing over his difficulties at Warwickshire, and helping him to integrate again into the dressing-room atmosphere.

I do not think one side got more out of the whole saga than the other. Packer got his exclusive rights, and the publicity given to Channel 9 only underlined the fact that he has the best television station in Australia. I do not believe he ever wanted to control world cricket: to him, it was always a local dispute, and a chance to get his own back on the Board after years of dispute. Meanwhile the control of world cricket stayed in the hands of the I.C.C., although the Australian Board seemed to be trying to get us to dance to their tune a little too much as the decade ended.

Things always seem clear-cut in retrospect, but cricket was ripe for a revolution of sorts in March 1977. Huge crowds had watched the big Centenary Test, proving once and for all that cricket was a big crowd-puller. While they poured into the Melbourne ground, the Australian players were moaning that the people who cleaned up the stadium were

IAN CHAPPELL

A rare photo of Ian Chappell in a benevolent mood – mind you, he had just captained the Australians to victory against England in 1975, and that would bring a smile to anyone's lips. A very strange individual to me, with a self-destructive streak, Chappell was one of the most influential cricketers of the decade. A very fine, successful captain and a world-class batsman, Chappell switched Australia's image into one that mirrored his own character – opportunist, ruthless, and mercenary. He had no time for stuffy talk about the traditions of Test cricket: I remember him chatting on all the way through the speech of Sir Donald Bradman at the official Centenary Test dinner in 1977. He seemed to have an obsession about Bradman: he was always running him down. I don't know whether it stemmed from the fact that they had both played for South Australia, or whether he was fed up with hearing about Bradman from his grandfather, Vic Richardson, who played with the great man on many occasions for Australia.

Chappell was naturally rebellious, but he took it to remarkable degrees, almost as if he had to prove himself all the time. His 'sledging' on the field was legendary, and umpires could never take anything for granted when he was around. I thought his performance in the Super Test Grand Final in 1979 was typical of the man. The World XI needed just four to win with plenty of wickets in hand, so Chappell decided to put an end to it. He took the ball, ran up off three paces and bowled the ball about ten yards wide of the stumps to finish the game. Then he ran straight off the field.

He had running battles with many players: Brearley annoyed him because he couldn't ruffle Mike's imperturbable calm, while Botham sorted him out characteristically by knocking him off a bar stool and bowling very fast at him on the field of play. Tony Greig rubbed Chappell up the wrong way during World Series Cricket days; but I was never sure how much of Chappell's remarks were of the Muhammad Ali type, designed to hype up the contest.

A prime agent in the Packer revolution, Ian Chappell has undeniably lived the role he has designed for himself. Unconventional, disrespectful and single-minded, he made the rebellious cult fashionable.

---

getting paid more than them. Within five years, Australia had gone from rock bottom to big box-office: a million and a half spectators had watched them thrash England and the West Indies in the previous two years, and the Aussie players, never the most diffident of sportsmen, were fed up. The small Test grounds in the West Indies meant there was never enough money to reward their players for their brilliance; once Clive Lloyd and Deryck Murray were won over there was a rush of West Indians queueing to sign up. Meanwhile the South Africans Procter, Richards, Barlow, and Pollock were disillusioned by the abortive efforts to get their country back into the Test arena, and Packer was a dream come true for them. Tony Greig's persuasive tongue was won over by dreams of money, influence and his fondness for Australia. He had always been very close to Amiss, Knott and Underwood, so England were going to suffer as well. The Pakistanis – who always seemed to be involved in pay wrangles with their Board – were no problem either. So the background for the coup was ideal. The game was being run by well-meaning, honest amateurs with conservative leanings, and they did not know what hit them.

It remains to be seen whether W.S.C. benefited Test players, other than bringing financial security to both the Packer men and those of us who stayed with the Establishment. Certainly the initial playing effects have not been impressive: too many batsmen look shell-shocked from endless ordeals by speed; too many fast bowlers are pitching it short, instead of trying to bowl batsmen out; and there is an underlying feeling that macho poses are now necessary in Test cricket. It is good that helmets have been popularized by W.S.C. – that is something I have advocated for a long time – but it bothers me that the use of helmets encourages fast bowlers to ping the ball round batsmens' ears all the time. After a while that gets boring. A lot of the grace seems to have gone out of Test cricket since Packer – and not just in terms of behaviour. A spin bowler was a rare sight indeed in Packer cricket and, since they returned to the Test arena, captains such as Clive Lloyd and Greg Chappell have shown little inclination to veer from the 'speed is everything' philosophy. As far as I am concerned, Test cricket will not be restored to proper health until the spin bowler again plays an important part in the winning or losing of matches. W.S.C. has done nothing to encourage that trend.

—4—

AUSTRALIA

FOR almost half the decade, Australia was the dominant force in world cricket. It was not just the results that made Australia so influential in the seventies – it was their style of play, and a revolution by their players, that were so crucial. W.S.C. stemmed from two main factors: the recent, dazzling success of the Australian team and their own simmering discontent at the lack of money that was coming their way. It led to the ultimate irony in March 1977: that, while the cricket world saluted the centenary of Test cricket between Australia and England, plans were being hatched during that historic match to set up a rival to

ENGLAND v. AUSTRALIA				
Season	Tests	Won by England	Won by Australia	Drawn
1970–1	6	2	0	4
1972	5	2	2	1
1974–5	6	1	4	1
1975	4	0	1	3
1976–7	1	0	1	0
1977	5	3	0	2
1978–9	6	5	1	0
1979–80	3	0	3	0

official Test cricket with the complete support of many current Australian players.

Ian Chappell was the main catalyst, both for the players' acceptance of W.S.C. and their hard-faced method of playing cricket that became known as 'sledging'. Chappell was such a fine captain, such a strong personality, so much a players' man, that his influence was bound to be a wide one with his team. Men like Walters, Lillee, Marsh, Mallett, Redpath and Walker had been together a long time; their leader was Ian Chappell. They followed his pattern of play on the field, turning a Test match into a war of nerves and gamesmanship. Their trust in him was so great that when he decided it was time to undermine Test cricket, inevitably the top players followed his lead.

I played Test cricket on five tours to Australia, and the difference in the atmosphere on the field was remarkable. On my first tour in 1970–1, the cricket was the traditionally tight and gripping brand. No quarter was asked or given – how could that be otherwise with Ray Illingworth and Bill Lawry the rival captains for most of the series? – but with great sportsmen like Graham McKenzie and John Gleeson in the Australian team, the relationship between the two sides was basically affectionate, with not too much sharp practice on the field. By the end of the decade – on Mike Brearley's second tour as captain – the relationships had been soured. Ian Chappell was back in the side, and Dennis Lillee was the acknowledged superstar with apparent licence to intimidate umpires and players and even throw in a quick commercial for his aluminium bat. Appealing at regular intervals was the norm and the England side – worried that they might miss a chance – followed suit. The umpires were under immense pressure, which the players did not help to relieve, and it had all got very opportunist. The Australians seemed to have perfected the practice of pressurizing the umpires; it seemed to me that we were all travelling down that particular road. Even the crowds had changed; in 1970–1, you could hear some genuine shafts of wit: 'Underwood, you're so slow running round the boundary you could read the adverts.' But nearly ten years later it was often a case of moronic chants of 'Kill, kill, kill' as Lillee ran in to bowl. The barracking of our players had turned into vulgar abuse as they fielded near the boundary.

The Australian Board's attitude to world cricket had also changed dramatically. Before and during the Packer Affair they had been constant in their support for Test cricket. The one-day stuff was gimmicky and a little vulgar, it seemed; indeed the Aussie players seemed to think

HISTRIONICS

A characteristically histrionic appeal by three men who perfected the art: Rod Marsh, Greg Chappell, and Dennis Lillee. Ian Chappell, no shrinking violet when it came to a full-throated and optimistic appeal, remains strangely passive at second slip. It seems almost anti-climactic to point out that this L.B.W. appeal against England's Bob Taylor at Melbourne in 1980 was turned down. Lillee's carefully orchestrated reactions whenever the ball happened to hit a batsman's pad were to me a byword for acting skills above and beyond the course of duty. He seemed to end up believing the publicity generated by the posters in this picture. Certainly a perforated eardrum became a real possibility for a batsman when Lillee, Marsh, and the Chappells were around.

so as well, because they never really learned how to play it throughout the decade. How else would five of them have managed to get run out in the 1975 World Cup final? It seems to me that the Aussie players often used the one-day matches for practice when they toured England. Until the Packer Affair, the Australian Board seemed simply to tolerate one-day cricket, with the traditionalist attitude that it does not do much for the development of Test players. On the 1979–80 tour the wheel had come full circle, and one-day cricket was on top. The Board had got commercially-minded because of the amount of money lost to the traditional game by the Packer schism. England, Australia and the West Indies careered round the continent for the sake of one-day cricket on that tour. The Australian Board had decided that was what the public wanted. To me, it was purely a commercial decision based on expediency, and successive touring sides there will probably have to get used to the same kind of tour, where Test cricket does not have the star billing. Yet only nine years earlier, we played the first one-day international on New Year's Day, 1971 – and all the officials, players and public I talked to at that time were convinced it would never catch on in Australia!

On that first tour of Australia, I was little more than a wide-eyed innocent. I was flown out to join the tour party in November when Alan Ward broke down with injury, and my lack of experience in first-class cricket can be gauged by the fact that I had never met my captain and vice-captain, Ray Illingworth and Colin Cowdrey. John Edrich was the man who pushed my claims to the management when a replacement was needed; I had played with John at Surrey, and he had always encouraged me just to run up and bowl fast. That is all I did during those Tests in Australia, although I learned a lot from experienced bowlers like John Snow and Peter Lever. I remember being shattered by the Australian heat, by the fact that we had to bowl eight-ball overs, and by having to stay in the field for a couple of days at a time. On the first day of my Test career at Sydney, I ended up completely exhausted, even though I had not set foot on the field during the entire day. I sat and watched every ball, hanging on the knowledgeable words of men such as Cowdrey, Illingworth, D'Oliveira and Fletcher. I have not changed much in that respect: I still worry enormously when my side is batting and I try to watch as much as I can.

The Aussies were hard, tough competitors, and they did me no favours when I walked in on a hat-trick in my first Test. I survived that, but didn't bowl too well. Ray Illingworth mothered me and boosted me with some Yorkshire blarney till, like the others, I just wanted to bowl my heart out for him. His captaincy was a real eye-opener to me. He seemed to have everything calmly under control and we simply had this feeling that everything would come good because Illy was there. He and his opposite number, Bill Lawry, were from the old school of captains who thought there was nothing wrong with settling for a draw, when the other side had a better chance of winning. (Things have not changed that much, I suppose!) So the first two Tests were pretty tedious affairs and our manager, David Clark, was clearly disgruntled at Illy's approach to the task. Clark belonged to the era of amateur captains and he embodied many of the traditional M.C.C. characteristics. When I first joined the tour I spent hours over dinner with him, and it was clear to me that he was fundamentally opposed to Illy's style of captaincy. It came as no surprise after the first two Tests, that Clark should say to the Press: 'I would rather lose the series three to nothing than have any more tame draws.' That was not the view of his players, and we were completely behind our captain. His policy was to hold things together and strike when the conditions gave us a chance to sneak a win. It worked twice – thanks to the bowling of Snow and the spinners Underwood and Illingworth, the batting of Geoff Boycott, and that indefinable thing called team spirit.

I do not think the Aussies had that same cohesion, even though their players were individually very skilful. Two significant events happened in that series: the start of Ian Chappell's reign as Australian captain and the début of Dennis Lillee. For the last Test, which Australia had to win to hold on to the Ashes, they replaced Bill Lawry as captain. More surprisingly, he was dropped as a batsman – an incredible decision considering his experience and form, which was still pretty good. Ian Chappell was given a very weak side, but he still made us fight all the way. Our spinners won a fascinating match, but one of the things that stuck in my mind was the way Chappell got things together right from the start. Bill Lawry had been a dour, unspectacular captain, playing it always by the rule book, but Chappell was dynamic, unorthodox and clearly a fine captain in the making. He had found his main attacking weapon: Dennis Lillee made his début in the Adelaide Test and immediately looked a terrific prospect. Naïve and inexperienced though I was, I could still see that he had everything a great fast bowler needs, and I could not help wondering how far I could go with my comparatively modest gifts.

That series was a controversial affair, even though relationships

51

between the two sides were generally very good. The umpiring appeared poor and indecisive, a constant problem in Australia, where the umpires simply don't get enough top-class practice. Ray Illingworth would lose no time in stating his opinion to the umpires, and this led to a couple of nasty moments. Lou Rowan warned John Snow for excessive use of the bouncer, when it was clear to most of us that Snow was bowling short of a length, but very fast, and within the spirit of the game. Then, in the last Test, Snow was grabbed by a spectator on the edge of the boundary and, with beer cans raining down on the field of play, Illy wasted no time in taking us off. That was perfectly correct, because we felt in danger; but that action did not exactly endear him any further to our manager. David Clark felt Illy had over-reacted, and heated words were exchanged. We went back on the field, but it was clear to us that Illy felt aggrieved by the lack of managerial support.

Although a great triumph for Illy on the field, that tour was a difficult one for him. He had taken over the England captaincy when Colin Cowdrey snapped his achilles tendon in 1969. Many thought it would just be a caretaker appointment, but he made such a great fist of it that he kept the job till 1973. Cowdrey was dejected at missing the captaincy for the Australian tour and, although he eventually agreed to go as vice-captain, he seemed disillusioned. His form – both with the bat and in the slips – suffered, and he spent a lot of time away from the team instead of doing the usual vice-captain's chores.

Things did not improve when an extra Test was organized without Illingworth or the players being consulted. The third Test over the Christmas period had been completely washed out, and the Australian Board, having lost a lot of money, wanted another one arranged. Instead of discussing the matter with the England captain, it was thrashed out by Sir Cyril Hawker, the M.C.C. President, and the M.C.C. Treasurer, Mr Gubby Allen – and David Clark. That led to players' meetings, angry exchanges of views, and final acceptance of the extra Test – but I do not think Illy ever forgot the way it was handled. Nor did any of us ever forget the words of the eminent cricket writer E. W. Swanton when we attended a dinner at Lord's shortly after the tour. We were under the impression that we had been invited for a celebration to mark the fact that we had regained the Ashes in Australia for the first time since 1932–3. Mr Swanton – not exactly an anti-Establishment figure – stood up at the dinner and told us that he did not like the way we had won. That echoed the sentiments made in a statement by the Cricket Council at about the same time, and so we

MY FIRST TEST WICKET

Sydney in 1971. Ashley Mallett caught behind by Alan Knott.

filed out with our tails between our legs as if we had let the game of
cricket down.

I don't think the Australians would ever take an attitude like that –
they just love hammering the Poms out of sight. I can just imagine Ian
Chappell sitting there, toying with his post-dinner brandy, letting a
member of the Establishment castigate his team for winning! E. W.
Swanton's words that night have often come back to me over the years
as Test cricket has got more intense, the acts of gamesmanship more
pronounced, and the physical intimidation greater. Compared with the
actions of certain sides in the seventies, Ray Illingworth's team was a
paragon of virtue. Significantly, there were no complaints from the
Australian players: they'd been tactically outwitted by a superb captain and a better bowling side. The Australians never waste too much
time in breast-beating about Test defeats. They get on with the job of
rebuilding, even if it means the departure of some fine players who are a
little past their best. Bill Lawry was ruthlessly cast aside in that final

Test, and both he and Graham McKenzie never played Test cricket again.

My first Test was Graham McKenzie's last, and it was sad to see this great fast bowler struggling; he had simply been worn down over the years, labouring away on dead wickets with little support at the other end. Graham's great physique was at once his major asset and his undoing: he would bowl for long spells and get lift and bounce from a flat wicket, while he would always run the risk of being over-bowled because his gentle nature did not allow him to tell his captain he was tired out. For all Graham's magnificent service, he was dropped as soon as he looked past his best. He may have needed barely a couple of wickets to overhaul Richie Benaud and become Australia's leading Test wicket-taker, but there was no room for sentiment. After all, the Aussies had another great fast bowler waiting to take over.

Dennis Lillee established himself as the best fast bowler in the world within eighteen months of his Test début. When he came to England with the 1972 Australian side, he showed that he had the priceless ability to move the ball around at high speed. He was the answer to Ian Chappell's prayers on that England tour; John Snow's dominance over them in 1970–1 was still fresh in their minds, and they were looking to Lillee to fight fire with fire if necessary. Lillee responded so magnificently that Snow was overshadowed, despite bowling splendidly throughout the series. Lillee also enjoyed crucial support from the other end for two of the Tests. It came from Bob Massie, a remarkable swing bowler who took sixteen wickets on his Test début. In the next Test at Trent Bridge he bowled John Edrich with one of the most astonishing deliveries I have seen: John, a superb judge of the line of a delivery, played no stroke to a ball that pitched a long way outside the off-stump, only to see it swing in devastatingly late and take the off-stump. That on a flat Trent Bridge wicket!

The England players involved in that 1972 series maintain there was something odd about those amazing performances by Bob Massie. Some of them agreed with Ted Dexter's theory that Lip-Ice, a greasy salve which keeps the lips moist, was used to make the ball swing. Dexter ran the story in a Sunday newspaper after Massie's two sensational Tests, after which Massie got just two wickets in the last two Tests, admittedly one of them on a spinners' wicket at Leeds. I'm sure we will never solve the mystery of Bob Massie and why he managed to swing the ball so astonishingly in two Tests, but the behaviour of his captain throughout the decade underlined that Ian Chappell was more pragmatic than most when it came to winning matches – and why did Massie decline so spectacularly after the Lord's and Trent Bridge Tests? He dropped out of his State team and when we saw him in Australia in 1974–5, he could hardly run up to bowl and his swing had disappeared. To be fair to Massie, his control at Lord's was astonishing, and during a 60-over spell in that Test, he made experienced, technically proficient batsmen such as Boycott, Edrich and Luckhurst look totally lost. He even contrived to bowl Mike Smith round his legs! The further irony was that at the other end Lillee bowled superbly, yet took just four wickets in the match. His time came, though – again and again.

That 1972 Australian side was an extremely formidable, aggressive unit. They were a mixture of youth and experience, with the Chappell brothers establishing themselves as world-class batsmen, Keith Stackpole invariably getting the innings off to a brisk start, a slimmed-down Rodney Marsh keeping wicket spectacularly and also batting pugnaciously, and the fielding – with Edwards and Sheahan outstanding in the covers – consistently brilliant. In contrast England had an ageing side, with such men as Parfitt, D'Oliveira, Luckhurst, Price and Illingworth, all hardly in the first flush of youth. England still had enough professionalism left to grab two victories on both occasions when the conditions favoured them – on the seamer's wicket at Old Trafford and the Leeds track that favoured Derek Underwood's unique bowling talents. Yet the dynamism of the Australian bowling and out-cricket was underlined by the fact that not one England batsman managed to score a century.

I played against the Australians for the M.C.C. at the start of the season, but then had to kick my heels for a time as I served out my qualifying period with Warwickshire. I had left Surrey because I saw no future for me there with Robin Jackman and Geoff Arnold getting the new ball ahead of me on merit, so I decided to move on. I had to serve a period out of the game, so I had plenty of opportunities to watch the Aussies in action that summer. I was twelfth man in the final Test at the Oval and, because of a series of injuries to England players, I spent a lot of time on the field. It was a great Test, with the Aussies needing 240-odd on the last day. Illingworth injured his ankle, Greig and Underwood did not bowl tightly enough, and Marsh and Sheahan batted sensibly at the end to win it. I fielded at short leg for long periods, and even picked up Ian Chappell off a mistimed sweep that hit his face and then lobbed to me.

ROD MARSH

Two pictures that sum up Rod Marsh, a great wicket-keeper, and the quality of Australia's umpiring. At Melbourne, Marsh appeals for a stumping against John Edrich, off the bowling of Ashley Mallett. He fails to impress the square-leg umpire, so turns his attention to Robin Bailhache at Mallett's end, who gives Edrich out caught behind, much to Edrich's astonishment.

Rod Marsh has been a tremendous performer throughout the decade. When I first saw him on the 1970–1 tour, he was overweight and a bit of a joke behind the stumps. We called him 'Iron Gloves', and Ray Illingworth used to joke that the backs of our heads were in danger when Marsh stood up to the spinners, because he was always dropping the ball. But Marsh lost a lot of weight, while still retaining the enormous power in his forearms that helped him to hit the ball long distances. His calf and thigh muscles were immense, and he could launch himself vast distances to take a high, bouncing delivery. The sight of Rod Marsh keeping to Lillee and Thomson on the 1974–5 tour was awe-inspiring, and the pounding his hands took was daunting.

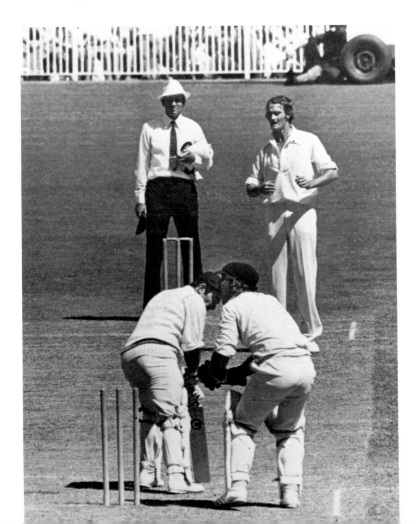

A fiercely competitive man, Marsh did not take kindly to umpires' decisions that went against him – or indeed the rub of the green. I recall sitting in the England dressing-room when he was out just after England had successfully managed to change the ball in the Edgbaston Test of 1975. Marsh was so furious at being outwitted that he took his anger out on the Australian dressing-room door, and reduced it to splinters.

I sat beside him at the official Centenary Test dinner, and I was struck by how much good sense he talked about the game and the way it was heading. Even then, he was heavily involved in the Packer negotiations, and I have often wondered if the vast sums of money his golfer brother Graham earned made him long for greater cash rewards from playing for his country.

When we won the Ashes back in 1971 at Sydney, Marsh was the first man through our dressing-room door at the end of the game. Then Test cricket got more serious for him, though I do not know how much he believed in the macho attitude adopted by Ian Chappell's team in succeeding years. Certainly Marsh always looked as if he meant business.

AT THE RECEIVING END

A picture that graphically sums up the fearsome danger of batting against Lillee and Thomson in those pre-helmet days. It is the fourth Test at Sydney in 1975, and Keith Fletcher has been hit on his cap after misjudging the speed of a delivery from Jeff Thomson – a fate that befell all of us on that devastating tour. It is hard to describe the frightening lift off the pitch that Thomson achieved in that series, although I am sure Keith Fletcher and others could try. This ball that rebounded from his cap was almost caught by Ross Edwards at cover – a fact that has not escaped the attentions of those arch-competitors, Rod Marsh and the Chappell brothers.

That last Test was full of prophetic omens for Australian cricket: centuries of contrasting styles but similar quality from the Chappell brothers; ten wickets for Lillee; brilliant catching and fielding; and aggressive, sensible batting to reach a difficult total. With Ray Illingworth limping out of the action on that last day, Basil D'Oliveira playing his last Test, and Geoff Boycott being absent from England–Australia Tests for the next five years, the balance was tipping Australia's way. Ian Chappell's authority as captain was total, and he was more than a match for the shrewd Illingworth. Chappell learned a lot very quickly, and by the end of that series Australia were on a course that was to take them to series victories over Pakistan, the West Indies (twice), and England, within the space of four years. He made sure that Australia played to its strengths, while overcoming chronic defects such as the lack of a settled opening partnership, the disastrous form of Doug Walters on England tours, and the moderate quality of their spin bowlers. Despite his good Test figures, Ashley Mallett never impressed me as a spinner: he picked up a lot of wickets against other countries, but I felt England always handled him well enough. He did not bowl many English sides out – but then that particular forte belonged to the Australian fast bowlers, and Chappell built his strategy round them.

That 1972 side contained some very influential men for the future of W.S.C. The shrewder players among the tour party noticed the large crowds at the Tests, and compared that fact with their lack of financial security. Once Ian Chappell had established a power base for himself with his team, he would waste no time in pressing his claims for extra cash for the side. He would do it with great vigour, not only because he believed in the justice of his cause, but also because he was fundamentally a bit of a rebel. Of that 1972 side, the Chappell brothers, Lillee, and Marsh were to be crucial playing cogs in the Packer wheel, Keith Stackpole and David Colley became TV commentators on Channel 9, Ashley Mallett became a pro-Packer journalist, Bruce Francis acted as Tony Greig's agent in the climactic Centenary Test period when the deal was set up, and Ross Edwards used his accountant's expertise to cost out the Packer operation when it was first discussed. Not only were the 1972 Australians an emerging side in cricket terms; they were beginning to realise their own commercial value.

Victories in the following year against Pakistan and the West Indies only helped to oil the superbly-drilled Australian machine, so that when England went out there in 1974–5, we were lambs to the slaughter. I was picked as England's main strike bowler, and we fully ex-

JEFF THOMSON

Jeff Thomson (pictured with his great friend and fellow-surfer, Len Pascoe) was one of the great sights of the seventies when his bowling was operating at full throttle. His speed off the pitch was fearsome, and his lift astonishing.

When I first saw Thomson bowl in the Queensland match in 1974, I immediately thought: 'What a sensible way to bowl.' He seemed to take very little out of himself with his javelin-thrower's action: no strain on the joints, no pounding down of the left foot, and little pressure on the hips or left knee. It was the first time I had faced a bowler and been frightened because I could not pick up the length of the ball. You saw the ball so late because he arched his back to deliver it from behind his right knee. The end product was terrifying. He and Dennis Lillee made a magnificent bowling combination that swept through England and the West Indies inside twelve months. Unfortunately, a series of injuries halted his progress; by the end of the decade, he looked unimpressive and a spent force. More than most great fast bowlers, Thomson needed rhythm: if he was worried about his run-up or some niggling injury, he could not rely on cunning like a Lillee – he was all-out pace or nothing.

A man with a typically Australian attitude to the outdoor life, Thomson loved fishing and all the other water sports. A fine all-round sportsman, he was totally different from his image. Sports writers imagined that he really meant it when he said he loved to see blood spilled by a batsman on the pitch, and when someone was stupid enough to pay him vast sums of money to say it on a radio station, Thomson happily obliged. In fact he was as good as gold, and never caused any trouble with the umpires. He would never make a fuss on the field, and perhaps this lack of Lillee-style aggression stopped him from being an even greater bowler.

Not the most intellectual of men, he contrived to flit in and out of the World Series Cricket project because he was short of money. A confirmed sun-lover, Thomson regarded cricket as only part of his life; but when everything was in proper working order, he was the most thrilling and dynamic of bowlers.

---

pected to be able to look after ourselves if the wickets were fast. Before we arrived in Australia, there had been lots of stories that Dennis Lillee was finished; he had struggled with a terrible back injury sustained in the West Indies and there were doubts whether he would play again. Max Walker had shouldered the burden in the West Indies and performed excellently but, after all, we were used to nagging, accurate medium-pacers like Max in county cricket. The name of Jeff Thomson

was mentioned in a few circles, but by all accounts he had not been very impressive against Pakistan, so we were not unduly pessimistic.

At first we did not know what had hit us. The wickets were generally green and under-prepared, and Lillee and Thomson just got more and more devastating. It was frightening to watch the ball rearing up off a length, and to this day I believe there was no way we could have played it. Only the very great – a Viv Richards, a Gary Sobers – could have tackled Thomson and Lillee in that series. The way Rod Marsh had to dive around for the ball showed how much bounce those two achieved; one of my abiding memories of the decade is the sight of Rob Marsh leaping like a salmon for deliveries that just took off, and of his throwing off his glove and cursing loudly when particularly quick deliveries bruised his hands. Thomson and Lillee were just too quick for our batsmen in that series – and don't forget, we had some good players of fast bowling in our team. Such men as David Lloyd, John Edrich, Dennis Amiss, Tony Greig, Brian Luckhurst, and Colin Cowdrey had faced up to fast bowling for years and none of them had ever experienced anything like it. It took men like Amiss and Lloyd several years to recover from their shell-shocked state.

I am told that many English cricket fans would sit and watch our batting from the comfort of their armchairs, and come out with statements like, 'Why can't they do better than just a tame shot to the slips?' The ball was on you so quickly that there was little that most of our blokes could do – though the lightning-fast eye and reflexes of Knott and Greig let them just step aside and carve it over the slips. You could not hook or pull these bowlers: they were just too quick for that. The following year the West Indies side, which had some of the best hookers in the world, was slaughtered 5–1 after they tried to carry the fight to Lillee and Thomson. There were no helmets available then, and I am sure many of our batsmen were scared – I certainly was.

Not only did Lillee and Thomson win matches, but they helped Ian Chappell's strategy. With Lillee restored to full fitness, Chappell could afford to go into a Test with just four front-line bowlers, because Lillee could bowl so many overs at speed. Max Walker would be brought on to give either of them a rest, then Mallett would bowl flat off-spinners for a time, and next thing you knew, Lillee and Thomson were back on. The game became static when England batted – the over rate was slow, and half the balls were either unplayably quick or wide, bouncing ones that we could not score from. The other deliveries were generally accurate, so that after an hour, you would look back and be able to think of about ten balls that we might have scored from. Our batsmen hardly saw a half-volley all day and, even when they did arrive, our blokes were so shattered from fending off the quick stuff that they were never in the right technical position to capitalize on a loose delivery.

Colin Cowdrey was flown out just before Christmas after Amiss and Edrich had suffered broken fingers. Colin was forty-three, but in county cricket he was still a fearless, calm player of fast bowling.

Within a couple of days of flying in he was facing the Aussies on a flyer at Perth. He battled away during the series, and certainly looked more assured than many of our other batsmen; but he found it terribly difficult to score runs. It was all very well staying in there and looking correct and well-coached, but eventually Chappell's tactics would just wear you down. I remember Colin struggling for about twelve runs in one Test after batting nearly two hours; Tony Greig replaced him when he was out and he proceeded to carve twelve in one over. God knows what Colin must have thought – despite his vast experience and enormous skill, he found the 1974–5 tour a different proposition.

We had no fast bowlers to give the Aussies a consistent taste of their own medicine. I played in five Tests but for a number of reasons – I still was not into a sensible training programme and I had injured knees – I couldn't make life uncomfortable for the Australians for very long. I remember a comment from Ian Chappell during that tour that stung me: he said that Willis was there for the taking after tea, because I simply was not fit enough. He was right, of course: I was put on a course of injections during the tour, but then my knees finally gave way at Adelaide in the fifth Test. It was to be another eighteen months before I could honestly say I was fit for bowling fast at the highest level. As for the other English bowlers, with only seamers such as Chris Old, Mike Hendrick, Peter Lever, and Geoff Arnold in our tour party, there was never any hope that we could bounce out the Aussies. Lever and I tried it on the first day of the series at Brisbane, and even though the wickets helped the quicker bowlers, we could never mount a sustained challenge.

It was a desperately bad time for Mike Denness to try to tighten his grip on the England captaincy. In my view, he was the wrong choice for the West Indies tour a year earlier, but on the Australian trip he had improved. Man-management seemed one of Mike's weaknesses, but this time he tried his best to get the team involved as a unit. His own batting form was so poor that he dropped himself for one Test, something I think the captain should never do because it undermines morale. I am afraid we never really took to Mike as captain: he did not seem to know how to gee up bowlers. A specialist batsman, he seemed to lack knowledge about bowling. He made a disastrous error in the fifth Test at Adelaide, when we were already 3–0 down. There had been no play because of rain on the first day and then, when play eventually started, Denness put the Australians in to face Underwood on a drying pitch. Soon they had lost five cheap wickets, and Fred Titmus was given an over at the other end. In that over, one ball turned and leapt over Greg Chappell's shoulder – yet Fred was taken off straight away, and Arnold and I were used to contain things while Underwood tried for a breakthrough at the other end. The Aussies could not believe their luck, as Fred bowled just seven overs in the entire innings. Somehow the Aussies contrived to beat us handsomely after we had had them 84 for 5 against Underwood on a wicket right up his street!

By that time, though, we were all pretty demoralized. We knew we could not live with Lillee and Thomson, while the Australian batsmen were playing well and their fielders caught everything. In fact, if Thomson had not missed the last Test through injury while Lillee could only bowl six overs, we might not have got our consolation victory at Melbourne. Dennis Amiss in particular breathed a sigh of relief when Lillee limped out of that last Test; he had fallen three times in a row to Lillee and he seemed utterly dejected by his psychological mastery over him. Amiss could not get over some of the language Lillee used to him in the first Test: 'Amiss, you're a . . . , and what's more, you're no . . . good as a batsman.' Eventually, Lillee could have run up and bowled an orange to Amiss and got him out, such was his hold over this fine batsman. For all of us, it took a long time to get used to the 'sledging' on the field of play. Lillee bowled me a beamer and hit me a couple under the heart when I tried to play him off the front foot and I got the treatment. Once on the field, it was as if he were drugged: he would strut around wild-eyed and glare at the batsmen. I suppose this was his way of geeing himself up; but in my view all these histrionics were unnecessary, considering his absolute splendour as a fast bowler. Lillee had delighted himself and all cricket lovers by making an amazing return after his back injury, and he seemed to have swallowed all the superstar stuff in this series. To my mind, he has been the same mixture ever since: a magnificent fast bowler, but with occasional appalling lapses of behaviour on the field that do not seem to be discouraged by his captain.

There were far too many verbal exchanges in that series, and only Tony Greig of the England side enjoyed them. Greig, an incorrigible extrovert, was quite happy to play up to the crowd and point to the dressing-room when he had dismissed an Australian; he would give as good as he got when the verbals were flying around, and the Aussies respected his competitive instinct and big-match temperament. He played really well on that tour, and in retrospect that was the time when he fell in love with Australia. He liked the brashness and the attitude to making money out there and during that tour he was clearly setting out his business stall. At breakfast, one would usually see Greig seated beside a couple of agents or financial advisers, going through the small print of business deals. At that time, commercialization of cricket was catching on, the Australians loved Greig, and he was in the right place at the right time.

We were not a happy outfit on that trip, and the atmosphere between the two sides was not very pleasant. Having said that, we were still expected to go next door to the Australians' dressing-room at close of play every day. I could not see the point of drinking with a bloke who had just tried to knock your head off and called you every name under the sun. So I would stand there, feeling rather embarrassed and trying to think of things to say. Eventually, I got thoroughly miserable with the tour, and fed up with the Aussies gloating at us. Many of our players had their wives and children with them, and the hotel seemed to be swarming with kids. It also made the guys that did not have their families with them very homesick. It cost so much to take a family out to Australia that to make it worth while they would have to stay for at least a month; but it did not help the team. Some of our batsmen would be up in the middle of the night looking after their children – then, a few hours later, walking out to face Lillee and Thomson.

I decided that I was going to do my best to enjoy the tour, once I saw the way the wind was blowing. We were being thrashed out of sight, my knee injuries were giving me some trouble, and the team spirit was very low; so I sought out the company of non-cricketers, and left my team-mates with their families. I felt sorry for Mike Denness: at that stage of the tour he was not worth his place in the side and he must have felt his position was being undermined by some of the senior players who had been very close on previous trips. All in all, it was a bad time for a captain who was never the greatest communicator among men.

The absence of Snow and Boycott did not exactly help us in this series, although I think that even with them we would still have lost. Snow was still a thoroughbred bowler, but the selectors were down on him for a variety of reasons. He should have been bowling for us on that tour; and his presence in the TV commentary box was deeply embarrassing for us all and, I suspect, for Snow himself. Boycott had pulled out of the tour because of mental pressures. I had no time for that attitude then, and still don't after all these years. My attitude is that you should go out there and try your best for your country, whatever the clash of personalities involved. It was obvious that Boycott disapproved of Denness's appointment as captain and, although he admired Greig, it did not help that he was a South African. As we travelled around Australia, fending off Lillee and Thomson on poor wickets, I got fed up with expatriate Yorkshiremen telling me what a great batsman Geoff Boycott was. That is an opinion I share, incidentally, and I disagree with those who say he was scared to face the quicks: he took some fearful punishment before and after, and I have never doubted his bravery. In 1974 he was our best batsman, and he should have been encouraged to go on that tour.

That 1974–5 series throws up so many memories that are still fresh: trying to find the wicket on a strip cut by the Lord Mayor of Brisbane on the eve of the first Test; Doug Walters hitting me for a massive six off the last ball of the day at Perth to reach a hundred between tea and close of play; Colin Cowdrey introducing himself in characteristically civilized fashion to an astonished Jeff Thomson when he walked out to bat at Perth; John Edrich battling through the England innings at Sydney with two cracked ribs; and the wonderful Australian slip catching – in the Perth Test, they took seventeen of the eighteen chances offered. There were the astonishing crowds: 77,000 packed Melbourne on Boxing Day. Test cricket was becoming big box-office in Australia and the home side were playing it the way the Aussies conducted their own lives – brashly, noisily and demonstratively, with scant respect for attitudes they deemed to be outmoded. This 'Ocker' philosophy had spread to Australian cricket and, as long as it remained successful, there would be no alteration in their style and method of playing something that was virtually no longer a game to many of them.

The Australians maintained that the wickets in England were 'doctored' in 1975 to draw the teeth of Lillee and Thomson. I am no expert on such things; but it is true that three of the four Test wickets (at Lord's, Headingley, and the Oval) favoured the batsmen, while the only one that helped the bowlers – a wet one at Edgbaston – led to a devastating Australian victory by an innings. It was a long, hot summer in 1975; and throughout the seventies, wickets in England have got slower and slower in dry weather, rather than speeding up as would be the case abroad. Whatever the reasons, the 1975 wickets helped England's strategy, which was an understandable one: to stop the rot.

Mike Denness was sacked after losing the first Test. He had won the toss at Edgbaston, and went round all the players asking their opinions. I was recovering from my knee operation at the time, and I sat in the

SYDNEY HILL

The flotsam and jetsam of the Sydney Hill during the 1975 Test against England. The Hill used to be a place where, although the paternity of English cricketers was sometimes called into question, there remained nevertheless a grudging respect for the good opposition players. That changed in the seventies. The 'Ocker' cult took over, encouraged by the histrionics of Lillee & Co., and it became a nightmare to field nearby. As the day wore on, the cans of beer would get emptied, then they would sometimes land on a head or two and the fights would start. Geoff Boycott suffered more than most from the Sydney Hill, and the situation got so bad that Mike Brearley rotated his fielders in front of the Hill. During the fourth Test of 1975, a total of 864,000 empty beer cans were carted away. Details of police arrests are not available.

dressing-room as the England lads advised Mike to bat. He chose to field, gambling against the weather forecast which promised heavy rain – and it all fell apart for Mike. We were caught on a wet wicket: Lillee, Thomson, and Walker took nineteen wickets in the match, and that was the sundown for Mike Denness. He was, of course, unlucky with the thunderstorm and the fact that Test wickets in England were still uncovered in those days. I remember the Aussie players saying during the game how ridiculous it was to leave a wicket open to the elements. I agreed with them that the luck factor in cricket comes with the toss of a coin, not with whether rain pours on to an unprotected wicket. Still, the Australians were not complaining, and it looked as if history was going to repeat itself a few months after our thrashing in their country.

But Tony Greig helped stem the tide. His appointment as England's captain pleased the Press, who wanted a glamorous, media-conscious character to lead from the front. The players were happy as well – apart from John Hampshire, who felt so strongly about a South African captaining England that he had to be persuaded to play in the third Test in front of his home Leeds crowd. At Test level, Greig was always worth his place in the side and, although his task came into the King Canute category, he did pretty well to give England back its self-respect for the rest of that 1975 series. David Steele was brought in to help blunt the onslaught, and his style of pushing forward with bat and pad close together frustrated the Aussies on those flat wickets. Bob Woolmer and John Edrich also grafted away during that series, but Lillee's dominance of Dennis Amiss continued – dismissing him three times out of four until Amiss was left out.

There is no doubt that Australia were the better side in that English summer. The wickets of Lillee, Thomson, and Walker cost a little more than in the previous series; but their effect on England's batting can be judged by the line-up in the Melbourne Test in February and the one in the Oval Test, six months later. None of the first five batsmen at Melbourne survived to the Oval. Another fine bowler was added to the Australian crop: Gary Gilmour. He wrecked the England batting in the World Cup semi-final at Leeds and he took nine wickets in his only Test that summer. A very talented cricketer, who fielded beautifully and hit the ball a long way, Gilmour unfortunately appeared lazy and a reluctant practiser. He could swing the ball prodigiously, with the gift of bringing it in late to trap the right-hander L.B.W. He was not all that quick but, when he signed for Kerry Packer, he kept out the redoubtable Len Pascoe for a spell. Unfortunately he did not keep himself fit enough and, when he struggled through the Centenary Test, he was dropped for the 1977 tour to England. If Gilmour's attitude to fitness had been right, he would have filled a role that the powerful Australian sides under the Chappell brothers never adequately covered: the all-rounder spot. They had any amount of bowlers who could bat a bit (O'Keefe, Jenner, Walker) and batsmen who could pick up useful wickets (Greg Chappell, Walters, Watson and Inverarity), but never in the seventies did Australia possess a Botham, a Boyce or a Kapil Dev.

Ian Chappell bowed out of Test cricket at the Oval, after captaining Australia for thirty Tests. He said he was tired of the strains involved, but in fact he was fed up with wrangling with the Australian Board. Whatever the rights and wrongs, this saga did not exactly mellow Chappell as a character, and it was typical of him that he did not acknowledge the Oval crowd's generous applause as he walked back to the pavilion after scoring 192. The macho image had to be maintained at all times. But, for all his faults, Chappell was still a very fine batsman, and his legacy to his brother was a strong, aggressive, Australian team. The players all knew what was needed from them on the field, and they made a point of psyching themselves up to hate the opposition as soon as they arrived at the ground for the day's play. Some of them – for example Max Walker, Ian Redpath, and Doug Walters – were very pleasant blokes over a beer afterwards, but at no stage was an Australian under Ian Chappell a soft touch. That corporate strength of character was too much for the West Indies a few months after the tour to England: they allowed themselves to be rattled by some bad umpiring decisions, and they simply folded up against Lillee and Thomson, with skilful support from Walker and Gilmour.

So the Australians still wore the crown of world champions when England arrived in Melbourne to play the Centenary Test. It is true that it sat a little awry: Thomson had been badly injured and his future was doubtful, while Lillee was having back troubles, and only a few weeks earlier the talented Pakistan side had thrashed the Aussies at Sydney. They were determined to take us apart in the Centenary Test: they played it like a Test Match, while we thought it was just going to be a big jamboree. We saw all those ex-players and great friends at Melbourne for the match, and we would have liked to have joined them for a few celebrations; but it soon dawned on us that the Australians meant business. We had had a very hard tour of India, then a fortnight of cricket in the heat of Sri Lanka, followed by a sixteen-hour flight to Perth. Just thirty-six hours after we had landed, we were playing

THE CENTENARY TEST

Two famous incidents from the Centenary Test.

Rodney Marsh calls back Derek Randall after Tom Brooks had given him out caught at the wicket. But after consideration, Marsh said he had not completed the catch when diving for the ball. It was a surprising gesture from Marsh – not the most Corinthian of opponents – and his honesty was rewarded when Randall was finally out shortly afterwards, having added another thirteen runs.

Rick McCosker's jaw is broken by one of my bouncers. My initial reaction was one of euphoria because I had dismissed a fine player – the ball came off his face and broke the wicket. I had no idea he was so badly hurt; but he showed his guts by coming out to bat in the second innings with his jaw strapped up, and he helped Marsh to add vital runs. That incident showed up the difference in our attitudes. If McCosker had been an Englishman, I have no doubt that he would have received a number of bouncers from Lillee & Co. when he came back in; but we kept the ball up to the bat so as not to aggravate his injury. Rick said, 'Thank you very much', and made twenty-five precious runs. We did not approach this game as a Test match, while the Australians played it like any side captained by one of the Chappells.

McCosker was never the same player after this injury, even though he made runs again at Test level. A pleasant, unassuming man, he was one of the more likeable Australians I played against in the seventies.

GREG CHAPPELL

Greg Chappell had a better image than his stormy petrel of a brother, but that was sometimes deceptive. When the mood took him, Greg could be as caustic as Ian. I recall getting a particularly virulent mouthful from him when I stood my ground at Melbourne in 1980, because I thought my snick to him in the slips had not carried. I reckoned that I had been unfairly given out in similar circumstances earlier in the series, and I waited till he confirmed the catch – which did not impress Chappell at all.

The complete antithesis to Ian in appearance, he would arrive at the ground looking immaculate, every inch the businessman, even down to the briefcase. Ian, on the other hand, would be outrageously casual, unshaven with tracksuit trousers on. I am still not sure which was the true identity of either.

Greg captained the side differently from Ian, preferring to lead by example, rather than blatant aggression; he also occasionally struggled to keep his temper on a tight rein. He should have cracked down on some of Lillee's outbursts on the field, but he appeared almost to sanction them. Greg's part in the notorious 'underarm incident' against New Zealand in February 1981 did not surprise me at all.

A beautiful stylist, he looked a class player right from the start of his Test career, when he made a hundred in his first Test against Ray Illingworth's side. He remained remarkably consistent thereafter. He had only one bad series – in England in 1975 – and that is something that happens to all great batsmen. Underwood troubled him on several occasions and, like most batsmen, he would occasionally get rattled by the bouncer.

Along with Barry and Viv Richards, he was the pick of the batsmen of the decade. In 1977, I admired the way he soldiered on as captain and the only class batsman in the Australian side. He looked tired by the middle of the tour, and I am sure the strain of that climactic summer affected his health; but he was sporting in defeat. He acted promptly to calm down Ray Bright when he was sure he had dismissed Boycott at Leeds that year; and it took a lot of dignity for Chappell to shake hands with Boycott an hour later, after he had on-driven him to get his hundredth hundred.

Chappell seemed to change in character whenever we played against him in Australia. He was far more aggressive than in England. Perhaps here he respected our umpires, and was happy to let them run the game.

against Western Australia. Most of us – including myself – were shattered, and the last thing we wanted to do was play a Test against Australia. That is why it did not mean all that much to me, although it was a fine game of cricket. Derek Randall played an innings that was remarkable for the shots he made and the way he outsmarted Lillee in the psychological battle; yet I could not believe it when Randall won the Man of the Match award. Lillee's bowling was magnificent: nearly fifty overs in the match for eleven wickets. Despite all the other fine individual performances, he won that Test. I could not help admiring the way he kept on bowling with a suspect back on a wicket that just got slower and slower.

I still was not fit enough at that stage of my career, and that point was hammered home to me at a barbecue a week later by my captain, Tony Greig. He said I could have won the Centenary Test if I had had the same attitude to fitness as Lillee. The real killer for me had been the second day of the match, when we had been bowled out for 95. That meant we faced a two-day stint of bowling on a slow wicket. I felt cheated by our batsmen because the bowlers had not got much-needed rest after doing so well on the first day. Eventually I could not summon up much enthusiasm for bowling. I realized I lacked the commitment and the pride in my performance of a Dennis Lillee. Soon I was to understand why Lillee had remained so committed to the cause for such a long period of time. He was about to line his pockets in a big way with Kerry Packer – and that is why he pulled out of the England tour a few months after Melbourne. During that Test he had decided to give his back a complete rest so he could be fit for the W.S.C. fray.

The 1977 Australian side in England missed Lillee. There is no doubt that their morale was badly affected by the rifts in the party over the Packer Affair. Their manager, Len Maddocks, was clearly embarrassed by the fact that most of his tour party were opting out of Test cricket in a few months' time to play for a rival organization. The non-Packer players in the party had a rough time: Kim Hughes only got into the last Test at the Oval, even though his batting record on tour was better than Packer men like Walters and McCosker; while Craig Searjeant was dropped after making a very impressive Test début with 81 at Lord's. For all the mental problems suffered by the 1977 Australians, the fact remains that England played very well indeed to beat them 3–0, and the only important absentee from the tour was Lillee – and he could not have done anything about their appalling batting.

We were lucky in our choice of captain. While Greg Chappell got more and more weary under the strains of the Packer trouble and the poor batting of his side, Mike Brearley led us with calm good sense. Tony Greig lost the job after admitting he was Packer's recruiting agent, but Mike, who had got very close to Tony, insisted he stayed in the team. That was right – after all, the Aussies were playing their Packer men, so why should we weaken our team by dropping Amiss, Knott, Underwood and Greig? So at the start of the series, Brearley called us together and told us to forget Packer for the summer. He was right to bind us all together like this, because the priority was to beat the Australians. They looked to be down at the start of the series, and those of us with long memories had no qualms about pushing them under. They would not have spared their breath expressing sympathy for England in a similar predicament.

Although Jeff Thomson bowled well, he was not quite his old self, perhaps because of his shoulder injury. Without Lillee, he lacked support at the other end, with Walker being overbowled and Pascoe only fitfully impressive. The Australian spinners – Bright and O'Keefe – simply confirmed their mediocre trend throughout the decade. Walters again failed in England; as soon as he came in, we would post extra slips and two gullies because he played across the line so regularly. He often took the bait. Hookes had arrived with a glowing reputation after hitting Tony Greig's undemanding off-spin for five successive fours in the Centenary Test, even though his overall innings was not that impressive. He did not last all that long in England: he was L.B.W. several times and, despite his consternation at the decisions going against him, he never had any idea where his stumps were because he moved around such a lot. The way Hookes reacted to successful L.B.W. appeals only served to underline the point that Ian Chappell's attitude to umpires had seeped through to a new generation of impressionable lads.

McCosker was never the same after I had broken his jaw in the Centenary Test, while batsmen like Ian Davis and Robinson simply were not Test class, despite their big contracts with Packer. The batting of Marsh fell away, and their fielding was in marked contrast to the brilliance of recent years. Rick McCosker's dropped catch off Geoff Boycott in his comeback Test at Trent Bridge was one of the significant moments between the two countries in the decade, while England seemed to catch everything. The diving effort by Tony Greig off my bowling to dismiss Marsh at Trent Bridge was one of the finest I have ever seen: a one-handed take from second slip position, ending up in front of Mike Brearley at first slip. There were two remarkable catches by Alan Knott at Leeds: one low in front of first slip, and the other a dive down the leg-side. The England slip fielders – Hendrick, Greig and Brearley – were outstanding, the outfielding of Lever and Randall was brilliant, and it was a marvellous all-round fielding team. I took a lot of wickets in that series through a combination of factors – better awareness of what I was doing, improved fitness, and bad batting – but the England fielding was one of the most important.

Ian Botham made his début for England, slotting into the side with supreme confidence and effect. Every change we made seemed to strengthen the team and, when Geoff Boycott was reinstated for the third test, we knew we had the Aussies on the rack. Boycott was not welcomed back with total warmth by the England side because some of us felt he should not have been brought back after dropping out for three years – but there is no doubt that England are a more difficult side to beat when he is there. Boycott was under tremendous pressure in that Trent Bridge comeback, especially after he ran out the local hero, Derek Randall. He just had to get a hundred then. He did so and, although he was not warmly applauded by the whole of the England side from our balcony, we all agreed he made the Australians' task even more difficult.

In the next Test at Leeds, there was a strong feeling that cricket history was going to be made on that first day. England had won the toss on a flat wicket, Geoff Boycott was on ninety-nine centuries, and the hundredth seemed there for the taking. I recall him saying to us before he went out to bat: 'If I can get to lunchtime, then I'll do it.' He has always felt that the balance of a Test is decided in the first few hours, so he sets his stall out to deny the bowlers. This he did and, in one of the most famous moments in cricket, he reached his century with an on-drive for four. His home crowd, of course, went wild, conveniently forgetting two controversial moments when it had seemed he was out. Early on he appeared to glove a Pascoe lifter to Marsh only to be reprieved; and then, when he was in the seventies, Bright was so convinced that Marsh had caught him on the leg-side that he went berserk at the umpire, Bill Alley, when the appeal was turned down. For me, the ultimate irony was the disbelief on the faces of the Australians, who had become the apostles of non-walking and gamesmanship. If the boot had been on the other foot in this case, they would have had no complaints.

Australia lost most of the tricks in that 1977 series. There was the time when Tony Greig deceived them into leaving out Pascoe and playing two spinners. He contributed a newspaper article the day before the Old Trafford Test, in which he said the wicket and the groundsman were a disgrace, that the ball would turn square very quickly, and that the toss would be crucial. So they played Bright and O'Keefe, Pascoe being made twelfth man despite an impressive performance at Lord's; but the ball didn't turn all that alarmingly, with the seamers picking up a few wickets on a good cricket wicket. Underwood got six wickets in their second innings, and his duel with Chappell was a classic; the wicket helped Underwood a little, but he always fancied himself a bit against Chappell, because he tended to lunge forward a little and give bat/pad catches, or to step away and try for the cut. He was out that way at Old Trafford, but not until he had made a superb century and I had deposited him on his backside with a fast bouncer. That last event was the more significant in the context of the series, because we noticed that Chappell did not like too many bouncers. Perhaps his nerve was failing, but I gave him a few after Old Trafford, and he was never the same batsman again in that series.

None of us felt sorry for Greg Chappell or any of his side. They were outclassed in every department, and it was good to be able to grind them down in the same way that they had played it in previous years. We had no idea what would happen to the shape of Test cricket by the end of the 1977 English season, for the air was thick with lawyers' writs and Packer hype. Many of Chappell's team looked distinctly lacking in class at the highest level – a fact that was borne out in W.S.C. – but that was their problem, not ours. Such players as Walters, Marsh, Thomson, and Chappell had great Test records, and we were delighted to have thrashed them out of sight. If, in the process, it had dawned on them that England were now a tougher bunch, so much the better. On the face of it, England looked as if it could stand the loss of key players to Packer better than Australia.

That point was underlined eighteen months later, when we beat Graham Yallop's side 5–1. Ian Botham had taken over Tony Greig's mantle of a class all-rounder, Bob Taylor had slipped smoothly into the gloves of Alan Knott (although Taylor could never match Knott's occasional batting brilliance), and Underwood's absence was balanced by the emerging skills of Miller and Emburey, while Gower and Gooch compensated for the loss of Woolmer's solid batting. Of the Australians, only Hogg, Hurst, Yallop and Hughes looked true Test class but, for all that, the series was a much closer one than the 5–1 margin indicates. Too often the Aussies would find themselves in a good position, but their dearth of all-rounders meant the tail would fold up, and they didn't react well to Brearley's pressure cricket.

The major differences between the two sides were in fielding and captaincy. It was the best England fielding team I can recall, with Gower and Randall brilliant in the covers and Brearley, Botham, Gooch, and Hendrick taking some blinding catches in the slips. Yallop's appointment as captain for Australia had much the same results as had that of Mike Denness of England: he couldn't get the players behind him and he relied on public school-style exhortations on the field. Rodney Hogg took the mickey out of Yallop all the time on the field, and very few realized he was doing it; Hogg was supposed to be a little dense, but I found him quite sharp, with a dry sense of humour. Like Jeff Thomson, he didn't believe in all this business of hating the batsmen and wanting to see their blood spilt on the pitch; but he'd go along with the image if it got more people watching the cricket. But Yallop could never handle Hogg; and, as a captain, it was very much a case of the professor and the schoolboy when comparing him to Brearley. Yallop has, however, been a good player for Australia, and the mere fact that Hookes and McCosker got into the Test side ahead of him in the following year proved that there was still a strong pro-Packer bias about their team when peace finally broke out between the two brands of cricket.

That 1978–9 series was a great one to play in because the sides were so evenly matched. The batting was generally weak, so there was always a good chance of a positive result. We were surprised to see our off-spinners pick up wickets, because Australian umpires have traditionally been 'not-outers' for L.B.W. appeals when the ball turns into the right-hander. The leg-side field for off-spinners has been a real bee in Australians' bonnets for years. They say it is defensive to have more than five fielders on the leg-side; they maintain that an off-spinner should bowl about eighteen inches outside the off-stump to an off-side field. But we feel that attacking bowling involves a leg-slip, a short leg and a short square leg for the off-break bowler, and then having some men out in the deep for the lofted shot with the spin. A classical off-spinner's field involves an 'in-and-out' field, and we did not see why we should compromise that, just because the Aussies did not like it. So their umpires would turn down L.B.W. appeals time and time again on previous England tours, so that men like Freddie Titmus would almost give up appealing when the batsman mistimed a sweep. But in 1978–9, after we refused to agree to a leg-side limitation, Miller and Emburey got several L.B.W.s and bowled sides out with attacking fields.

Although the umpires were fairer in their attitude to L.B.W.s from off-spinners, they were poor on that tour and worse the following year. I am a great believer in trying to help the umpire in his difficult job by walking if you know you have got a nick and only appealing if you think it is out. But the Australians make life very difficult for the umpires: on that 1978–9 tour, we soon saw the way things were going by the amount of times John MacLean behind the stumps and Gary Cosier in the slips appealed for ridiculous things. We came to the conclusion that the sheer volume of appeals would wear down the umpires, that they would crack and start giving them dismissals on a rota basis – for example, one success every five appeals, whatever their merits. So many of us did the same, and the result was that the air was thick with appeals throughout the series. Poor Tom Brooks, the best of the Australian umpires, was hounded out of the game after the Perth Test; a decent, honest man, he would be the first to admit he had a bad game at Perth, and the worst decision he gave was when he said Graeme Wood had nicked one to Bob Taylor off John Lever. I was at mid-off, so I had no idea about the merits of the appeal, but I understand Wood was a long way from the ball. After a long pause Tom gave him out, and the batsman couldn't believe it. The next day, the papers were full of Wood's outburst about Brooks's bad decision and, although he re-tracted his remarks later, the damage was done. Brooks retired from top-class umpiring, and I do not blame him. The Aussies in particular had made life difficult for him, and Australian cricket's attitude to umpires only succeeded in hounding out its best man. I was very sad about that.

The crowds had got even more abusive since our last trip to Aus-tralia. In 1978–9, Geoff Boycott was treated dreadfully by many spec-tators when he fielded on the boundary: they would throw things at him; gloat about him being sacked from the Yorkshire captaincy; even make tactless remarks about his mother, who had recently died from cancer. They behaved abominably, and it reflected great credit on Boycott that he did not lose his temper with them. When they won the Melbourne Test, the crowd were even more cruel and gloating and it gave us great pleasure to win the series by such a large margin, if only to stop some of the moronic Aussie spectators calling us 'no-hopers' and 'whingeing Poms'.

During that year, we had the unique experience of matching the traditional form of Test cricket against the razzmatazz of Packer's version. We were conscious of trying to do for 'fair dinkum cricket' what Bobby Simpson and the Indians had managed a year earlier, and I feel we proved that we were playing the right brand of cricket. Packer's minions pointed out that attendances for the Tests were greatly reduced compared to the golden years of 1974–7 in Australia, but that neglected the fact that Aussies will not come to see their side thrashed. If the scores had been reversed in that 1978–9 series, the grounds would have been packed. Anyway, I think the Australian

NIGHT CRICKET

The changing face of cricket: night cricket at the Sydney Cricket Ground, while the punters stretch their legs on the Hill. When it was first played in the 1978–9 season, night cricket attracted a fairly motley band of beer-swilling characters, many of whom preferred trying to break each others' skulls to watching Kerry Packer's players perfect their skills under the lights. World Series Cricket maintained that was simply Establishment propaganda, but the following season Mike Brearley – not the most emotional or pessimistic of men – warned that unless crowd excesses at Sydney were curbed, somebody would be killed.

Board make a mistake by starting off a Test series at small grounds like Brisbane and Perth. Brisbane is a lovely place to play but it can only hold 15,000, while Melbourne can easily take up to 80,000. In my view, Melbourne should be used for two Tests every series, now that the Australian Board has got heavily into the money scene.

I suppose our minds were closed to Packer on that tour, although few of us were impressed with any of the W.S.C. that we did see, apart from night cricket and the quality of the TV camera work. We wanted to play the series as a normal Test series, and we were quite happy to be in direct opposition to Packer, because we felt we had the superior product. I think Mike Brearley and Phil Edmonds were the only ones with a sufficiently open mind about W.S.C., but we were all happy to do a lot of public relations work to boost the Establishment line.

I would love to have seen the England side of 1978–9 matched against the Australian team of 1979–80. We didn't do ourselves justice at all against Greg Chappell's team, and that wasn't just because he had the Packer players at his disposal. Men like Kim Hughes, Alan Border and Geoff Dymock were non-Packer players from the previous year, but they'd matured as Test players in a short space of time. I had a disastrous time with the ball, Derek Underwood didn't make as big an impact as we hoped, our fielding deteriorated, and our batting just was not solid enough. The return of Lillee of course made a big difference, although Hogg and Thomson were shadows of their former selves.

We went on that tour with misgivings because we felt that a second visit within a year was robbing Tests against Australia of a certain magic. That is why I thought it right not to put the Ashes up for grabs, because this was a one-off series, hastily arranged to make the Australian Board some cash after the expensive Packer Affair. No doubt

81

the Board reminded Lord's that they'd agreed to the expensive litigation against Packer in the High Court, so we were honour-bound to do the trip. But the itinerary was absurd: the mixture of one-day internationals and Tests just didn't work, and the travelling was exhausting. All we seemed to do was check in and out of hotels and go to a cricket ground. Everything seemed so familiar to us after the previous year: as vice-captain, I would try to motivate our players with words like, 'Come on, we've got to get stuck in this session', and I'd look round and see the same old faces I had said the same words to about eight months before.

Things were not so happy for us off the field, either. Although Mike Brearley had a much better time of it as a batsman, he did not seem to get on personally with the manager, Alec Bedser, and had his cricketing disagreements with the assistant manager, Ken Barrington. Ken wanted to sort out the techniques of some of our young batsmen, an opinion I shared, but Mike would not allow it. He felt that if you are good enough to play for your country, then you are able to sort yourself out. Judging by our efforts, that was patently not on, but Mike would not budge. He did not quite get on the same wavelength as Alec Bedser, an old-fashioned character with a strong sense of tradition who was a fan of hard work in the nets. I think Mike missed the subtle, dry wit of Doug Insole, the manager in the previous year. I spent a lot of the time trying to bridge the gap between Mike and Alec. As vice-captain, I was frustrated because I was involved in electing a side for a Test when I had not been involved when the tour party was picked. When you have no say in the shape of the tour party, it can be difficult to be dispassionate if you have got a poor opinion of players who are in contention for a place in the eleven.

Because we weren't winning many games, it was inevitably an unhappier tour for England. There was no continuity of cricket: we switched between night matches and Tests; and often I did not know whether I was coming or going. There were problems and disagreements – especially at Sydney, when Geoff Boycott declared himself unfit just before the second Test. The wicket was wet and the start had been delayed, when Boycott came back from an indoor net to announce that his neck was still stiff. Poor old Wayne Larkins was alerted to the fact that he might have to make his Test début at fifteen minutes' notice against Lillee on a wet wicket, while Brearley told Boycott that ninety per cent of him was better than one hundred per cent of Larkins. I told Boycott to his face that he should be sent home right away; then

Brearley said to him, 'You're playing, and that's the end of it.' It was –
but even with Boycott we lost. That Sydney Test was just a lottery; I
think we all felt that whoever won the toss won the game, and Greg
Chappell was honest enough to say the same.

We made some selection mistakes for the first Test: Miller wasn't fit,
although he told us his back injury was not troubling him. We missed
Hendrick, who had to fly home with a shoulder injury. We were wrong
to open with Randall, instead of picking Gooch, who had had some
trouble initially with the short-pitched ball that came into him. He kept
popping it up to short leg, but hard work in the nets helped him over
that. But it was wrong to assume that Randall – with his nervy, jumpy
technique – could survive against Lillee, Dymock and Thomson as an
opening batsman. We made the usual mistake of picking a man for
Tests on the strength of good performances in one-day internationals –
in this case Peter Willey. Only Boycott among our batsmen impressed;
he practised devotedly for long hours, and he showed the sceptical
Aussies what a fine player he is. David Gower was very disappointing
after his success in the previous year. His 98 not out at Sydney was to
me an overrated innings and he could have been out a dozen times
before he reached fifty. He did not seem enthusiastic about net practice,
and the quickies got to him. On the previous tour Hogg and Hurst had
pitched the ball up a lot, which suited Gower's front-foot style; but in
the 1979–80 series, he was troubled by the short-pitched stuff on or near
his off-stump. Pascoe and Lillee did not give him much to drive, and as
a result he did not look a very good player.

Derek Underwood bowled well on occasions, with hardly any luck,
though he still troubled the Chappell brothers. But players like Hughes
and Border, who had not played much against him, were quite prepared to go down the wicket and hit him over the top – and I have not
often seen that treatment handed out to Underwood.

I did enjoy night cricket. It looked great on television, and there was
real atmosphere on the field. It was like being under the spotlight in a
rock concert, even if the stadium was not full. We got a predictable
amount of stick from the Aussies because we did not want to wear
striped coloured clothing or play with circles limiting the fielders in
certain areas. We thought them both too gimmicky, and Mike Brearley
was abused long and loudly by many spectators who were outraged by
his calmness and ability to discuss a case rationally. They thought
about ways to abuse Brearley: with his batting on the upgrade they had
to think about something else, so they fastened on to Mike's beard. He

became known as 'The Ayatollah', and the baiting and the catcalls followed him.

As far as I am concerned, the standard of umpiring reached an all-time low for Australia on this tour. The fact that a man umpired a Test in just his fourth first-class match just about sums it all up. The public loved to see Lillee turn round to an umpire with both fingers pointing at him following an optimistic appeal. He knew that the more he tried it on, the more chance he had of getting his way. Lillee's performance with his aluminium bat in the Perth Test took my breath away, not only for its cheek, but also because the umpires were so weak with him. He should have been disciplined under Law 46, which is an all-purpose regulation, covering unfair play in the umpire's opinion.

The funniest quote I heard about Australian umpires came from a well-meaning Aussie during that tour: 'You can say what you like about our umpires, but they're the best turned out in the world.' Quite so – and it only seemed appropriate that the bane of umpires, Ian Chappell, should still be alive and kicking as the decade during which he had consistently abused umpires drew to a close. We had a taste of Chappell's nonsense in the South Australian game, where he disagreed with the umpire for calling 'dead ball' when he was batting, then made a point of throwing a sweater in the same umpire's face when he was in the field, and finally put nine men on the leg-side when bowling to Brearley, to underline both his contempt for Brearley and his obsession with a leg-side restriction on fielders that England did not support. Chappell carried on in much the same way when he came back for two Tests, and I for one was heartily sick of him by the end of the tour. He hadn't changed; yet, even though some Australian players complained about his behaviour during Sheffield Shield games, the fact remains that he was still named 'Player of the Year' by the Australian State cricketers, so he cannot be that unpopular. Throughout the decade Chappell's influence on that Australian side has been obvious, even when he hasn't been playing.

By the end of that tour, I felt genuinely worried for the well-being of Test cricket. It seemed to me that it was being cheapened by the desire to make money out of the one-day brand. I don't believe such a concentrated programme involving England, Australia, and the West Indies can work: it's too arduous and repetitive, so that little by little the magic of Test cricket keeps getting chipped away. Night cricket appeals to a certain type of person – certainly not to a purist – but in Australia, the floodlit game could well get more and more popular at the expense of the established version. In Australia, money is an important ingredient in any equation, and the TV moguls will give the public what they want, irrespective of tradition. There is no sentiment in Australian sporting circles, and if more cash can be made out of the new wave of cricket, so be it. I think administrators like Ray Steele and Bob Parrish have the interests of the game at heart, and I am impressed by the younger breed like David Richards. I hope they will support England when we try to get the next itinerary for an Australian trip back to its more traditional format of four or five State games before the first Test, so that we can have a chance to find our feet, instead of rushing around all over the country.

Although Packer won the right to promote and televise Test cricket for a number of years, the Board are still very much in control of Australian cricket. That is why I was so disappointed when Dennis Lillee got off scot-free for his aluminium bat nonsense. He was simply reprimanded because, officially, no dissent had been reported by the umpire. I suppose it was Lillee's spirit of goodwill that caused him to throw the bat away when Brearley insisted it should be changed because it was denting the ball? Perhaps the Board realized that Lillee was great television and they couldn't afford to have him suspended from prime-time viewing.

One of my main worries is that the players will be burned out if the need to play more and more international cricket in Australia takes hold. For example, Kim Hughes seems to have been playing non-stop since he got into the Australian side in 1977. It would be nice to see Kim Hughes prosper as Australia's captain. I like him very much: he is a throwback to the McKenzie kind of Australian Test player. Kim genuinely loves Test cricket, he enthuses about it, and I have never seen him stoop to a low or shabby trick. Perhaps the example of men like Kim Hughes will usher in a new era of Australian Test players, far removed from the Ian Chappell image.

——5——

NEW ZEALAND

NEW Zealand advanced as a cricket nation in the seventies. They notched up their first wins over Australia and England and celebrated the dawn of the eighties by winning a series against the West Indies for the first time. Throughout, they basically remained charming blokes to play against, although they got more competitive as the decade progressed. For that, county cricket in England takes some of the credit: John Wright, Geoff Howarth, Richard Hadlee, John Parker and Glenn Turner all became better players after testing their skills and temperament in daily cricket. That is something they just can not get in New Zealand; of course, they try hard to be professional in their outlook, but it is difficult when many of their top players work during the week and play only at the weekend. In New Zealand cricket the money just is not around to boost professionalism, and that is why their best cricketers come over to England.

This essentially amateur aspect is summed up by the case of Glenn Turner, easily New Zealand's best batsman of the seventies. Early in his career he took a professional decision to improve his batting by playing in county cricket, while at the same time trying to carve out a secure financial future for himself. So he made himself unavailable for six Tests against England in 1978 because he wanted to play for Worcestershire during the benefit season. Many will castigate him for that, but it's possible to see Turner's point of view: he had had his wrangles with the authorities back home, and there was no justification for thinking that he would be welcomed with open arms, on account of his tendency to speak his mind on cricketing matters. The lack of financial incentive in his own country meant that he had to take a hard-headed attitude to his benefit. Whatever the rights and wrongs, there is no doubt that it is a fundamental weakness of New Zealand cricket which has partially led to a great batsman not playing for them in Tests since 1977.

The Kiwis have always been happy lads to play against. They would take their defeats with a good grace, possibly because for a long time it

ENGLAND v. NEW ZEALAND				
Season	Tests	Won by England	Won by New Zealand	Drawn
1970–1	2	1	0	1
1973	3	2	0	1
1974–5	2	1	0	1
1977–8	3	1	1	1
1978	3	3	0	0

had been ingrained in their subconscious that they were going to lose anyway. By the end of the seventies, they had five or six Test-class players; yet, although they had toughened up, defeat still wasn't a possibility they could ignore. John Wright, Lance Cairns, and Mark Burgess are great ambassadors for their country, and I remember how well they took the beatings on the 1978 tour of England. On paper it looked the best New Zealand side to tour these shores, but they never did themselves justice. That didn't stop them enjoying themselves and putting a brave face on things – like the time at the Oval, when, after losing the first Test, they joined us in champagne celebrations in our dressing-room, even though they faced a six-hour trip to Torquay that night for a game the following day. I can well understand why they were so bitter at the behaviour of the West Indians, when only one man turned up for the presentations at the end of the historic Dunedin Test, after the Kiwis had beaten the world champions by one wicket. The West Indians had the sulks about the umpiring, yet Richard Hadlee summed up the New Zealanders' feelings when he said that they had always felt an obligation to attend such ceremonies, even though they'd been on the receiving end of a thrashing often enough.

Cricket faces an uphill struggle in New Zealand, where rugby is the number one sport. Even when their deadly rivals Australia play there, they don't draw the crowds, and the W.S.C. tour in 1978 was a disaster, with the wickets poor and interest minimal. Just one small point illustrates the way cricket is viewed by the public over there – and, in

87

RICHARD HADLEE

Richard Hadlee was one of the most underrated bowlers in Test cricket during the seventies. He has a good approach to the wicket and a whippy action, with the commitment to throw himself forward on delivery of the ball. He often looks exhausted, and although he acknowledges his debt to English county cricket, he admits that its rigours have been a great physical strain. In an era that became increasingly dominated by pace, Hadlee gave his side definite firepower; and it was a pity that he lacked consistent support at the other end. Like all fast bowlers he had an ego, and it often needed massaging by his captain. Mark Burgess seemed particularly sympathetic in this respect. He needed to be psyched up a little before he started bowling, and I suspect Dennis Lillee taught him a thing or two in that direction when World Series Cricket took Hadlee as a guest player on their short tour of New Zealand.

A positive man on the field, Hadlee took on Ian Botham in the psychological stakes and lost heavily. Botham never forgave himself for getting out to Hadlee off a loose hook shot in the Wellington débâcle, and he set out to dominate Hadlee for the remaining five Tests against him in 1978. He hooked Hadlee out of sight many times thereafter – and when it was Botham's turn to bowl, Hadlee would be in danger of treading on the square-leg umpire's corns. He did not exactly stand up to Botham, preferring the slash to third man to the forward defensive shot, and soon Botham established a mastery over him that was only surpassed by the Lillee–Amiss combination. In fact, Hadlee's feat of doing the double in Tests surprises me, because I have always judged him to be more of a specialist bowler – and a very fine one at that.

telling the story, I am not trying to denigrate the friendly folk of New Zealand in any way. When we landed at Auckland in 1978 after the long haul from Karachi we had to carry our own bags and equipment around at the airport. Now, as grown men with plenty of strength in our shoulders, that may well be right and proper, but on every other tour I have been on with England, all that was taken care of by officials only too eager to help. In a place like India we would be treated like demi-gods, and many cricket fanatics at the airports would beg to carry our gear. But in New Zealand, we were only cricketers. If we had been there to play rugby against the All Blacks, I reckon things would have been different.

The climate is similar to England's, with plenty of cool summer days and rain. So the wickets resemble English ones in character; Eden Park

at Auckland is usually a good wicket after being lively on the first
morning, while Christchurch varies from green and bouncy to pretty
flat. Wellington has been reconstructed: when they beat us for the first
time in a Test, that Wellington wicket was like a park pitch. Our
batting was dreadful, but the pitch didn't help.

But it is depressing to play cricket on nothing but rugby pitches. The
outfields are invariably bad, which is not surprising when you consider
that hulking great sheep farmers run up and down on them with a rugby
ball for more than half the year. The dressing-rooms are very sparse
and functional, which is fine if you are only there for an eighty-minute
rugby match, but bad news if you are involved in a five-day Test. As a
result, you do not feel much atmosphere or excitement in a Test in New
Zealand. The television coverage is poor, with mediocre camera work

and banal commentaries, although the radio ball-by-ball commentary is not too bad. The Press pay lip service to cricket, but there is an underlying feeling that the New Zealand public are just marking time for the next rugby season. It does not help that most touring sides who come there are at the end of an arduous trip, having put in a few months elsewhere. They are jaded, and many just go through the motions.

That was certainly the case on my first visit there in 1971. The weather was poor, the crowds were sparse, and the atmosphere was non-existent after the heady days of Sydney a few days earlier. We'd already played six Tests in Australia and even the keenest players in our squad were shattered and longing for home. As for me, I was done in: it took me months to recover from that whole tour, and I walked around like a zombie even when I got back to playing for Surrey in the summer of 1971. So I was in no physical or psychological state to play when we got to New Zealand. I missed the first Test, and then John Edrich did his best to snap me out of my lethargy in the Auckland Test. He told me to stop bowling medium-pace, and to get stuck in because it was a Test match, and that all the wickets count in the record book. Typically sensible words from Edrich; but it was difficult, especially as the game was grinding on to a boring draw.

The previous Test had been a bonanza for Derek Underwood, who enjoyed himself on a dreadful wicket that turned from the word go. But what I remember most about that Test was the decision to give consolation caps to Bob Taylor, Ken Shuttleworth, and Don Wilson. Team spirit had been so strong on that tour that Ray Illingworth wanted to reward everybody with at least one game in New Zealand, so Bob Taylor took over from Alan Knott. Now Bob had been a loyal, uncomplaining reserve keeper who did superbly every time he had a chance on that tour, but he couldn't hold a candle to Knott, whom I never saw keep wicket better than on that tour. It was wrong to hand out prizes for being a good boy, and I think Bob Taylor was embarrassed by all of it. Alan Knott was angry about it, because he had his professional pride and didn't see why he should be rested. As I shared a room with Alan during that period of the tour, I can vouch for the forthrightness of his views on the subject! Imagine that happening later in the decade, when every Test throughout the world became an important event, both in money-earning potential and playing prestige.

I missed out on the 1974–5 trip to New Zealand because I needed a knee operation back in England, so I missed Keith Fletcher's double hundred and Tony Greig's ten wickets which gave us the first Test by an innings, with the second a rain-affected draw. The next time I went there was after the 1977–8 Pakistan tour, the most boring one I have ever been on. The cricket in Pakistan had been disappointing, the wickets so lifeless, and the overall atmosphere so low-key that we all went on a great blow-out for the first few days in Auckland. It was like entering paradise after the deprivations of Pakistan: we could drink milk again, eat salad and fresh meat, and savour the oysters. We all put on a lot of weight in the first few days, but we were soon jolted out of our euphoria by that defeat at Wellington.

Brian Rose had gone on to Wellington, and he warned us that the wicket looked dodgy. We only needed 130–odd to win, and I remember saying to our batsmen: 'Come on, we are not going to be the first England side to lose to this lot, are we?' We were – I went back to the hotel to have a bath because I was so stiff after bowling in a typical Wellington wind, and I was hastily summoned back when we were 38 for 6! Richard Hadlee and Dick Collinge bowled us out for 64 and mine was the last wicket to fall – appropriately enough caught at slip by my old mate, Geoff Howarth, a man I had spent many happy days with at Surrey. All credit to the Kiwis; but it was a disgraceful batting performance by our side, all of whom had batted on equally bad tracks in England. We relied too much on Boycott, who had taken over the captaincy after Brearley broke his arm, and the crucial dismissal came when Collinge bowled him with a big inswinger. After that, we folded like a pack of cards. Great was the euphoria in their dressing-room, and I am pleased to say we did our bit in the sportsmanship stakes; but I could not help feeling that there should have been more public joy at this historic victory. After all, it was the first time they had beaten England in fifty years of trying – yet the crowds were only about 4,000 a day, with hardly anybody turning up on the final morning to see us rolled over. In similar circumstances in India, Pakistan or the West Indies, a public holiday would have been declared, and the attitude of the Australians towards beating the Poms can only be imagined!

Geoff Boycott was blameless as captain in that Wellington Test, and he handled the Press very well indeed. But in the next Test our relationship took a turn for the worse, and it has never been right since. In that Christchurch Test we failed to make them follow on, and Boycott took it badly, as we all did. Late on the fourth day – with one day left – we batted again, 180-odd in the lead. The priority was quick runs, but unfortunately Brian Rose was out of form and Boycott was also struggling. As vice-captain, I thought it my responsibility to change the batting order and sent in the hard-hitting Ian Botham at number four. He proceeded to run out Boycott by about sixteen yards. When Boycott came into the dressing-room, he didn't say a word, but sat in a corner with a towel over his head. Phil Edmonds asked him about the rest of the batting order, and he said that it now appeared to be the responsibility of the vice-captain.

The next day, I mentioned to him that we would presumably declare at our overnight score to give us a complete day to bowl them out and square the series. He replied that, having already lost one Test, he did not want to lose another. I told him there were fifteen other blokes in the tour party who wanted to win the game, and he went off and did three laps of the ground chatting with Geoff Cope, his Yorkshire team-mate. Boycott did declare, though; and we bowled them out with time to spare and the captain gave all the credit to his bowlers. But I was annoyed at Boycott because, as vice-captain, I was perfectly entitled to try to take some of the weight off his shoulders. I doubt whether our manager, Ken Barrington, gave Boycott a glowing end of tour report, and I think that tour effectively ended Geoff Boycott's chances of ever captaining his country again. To be fair to Boycott, I could sympathize with the frustration he had felt through the tour, having to bat with the budding young players who lacked his expertise and professionalism.

Ironically enough, I captained England for much of the third Test over six days at Auckland because Boycott had trouble with his eyes. It was a terribly boring game on a very flat wicket. Clive Radley batted interminably for his hundred, Geoff Howarth made two centuries in the match, and for most of the time I bowled our spinners, Edmonds and Miller, in an effort to make the game more interesting. Everybody worked hard, but my abiding memory was that we all just wanted to get home. In fact, the main thing that sticks in my mind about that Test is that I managed to see my idol, Bob Dylan, in a brilliant concert at Western Springs. Again, though, the problems of tacking on a trip to New Zealand after playing elsewhere cropped up: we were all jaded, and we were conscious that we could have done more for Test cricket in that country if we had been fresher. It would be nice to send an England team to New Zealand before they played Tests elsewhere on their tour.

I always looked forward to meeting up with the Kiwis when they came to England. They really enjoyed themselves on tour, and it must have been a novel, exciting experience to be able to play cricket every

GEOFF HOWARTH

Geoff Howarth has been one of my best friends in cricket. We started together with Surrey, and we used to lend each other money if either one was down on his luck during those winters when the dole office or a petrol-pump attendant's job beckoned. Geoff stayed with my parents for quite a time in those early days, and our family links have always been strong.

I helped Geoff establish himself in Test cricket at the expense of my own England side. In 1978, his captain, Mark Burgess, asked me to have a talk with Geoff, because he had not fulfilled his undoubted potential and was in danger of being dropped from the Test side. I earbashed him at a party and told him he must concentrate more, and cut out all those airy-fairy shots. He became a more disciplined player, took three hundreds off England in the next four Tests (plus a 94), and ended up captain of his country.

Although now consistent at Test level, he has never turned in the goods regularly with Surrey. Domestic problems have had a telling effect on his batting, and I only hope that Surrey will keep faith with him for a little longer.

day for several months. An English professional will not shed too many tears if it rains at a particularly busy time of the season when there is nothing on the game – but the New Zealanders were always praying for good weather, because touring and playing cricket was such fun. They were great lads for sing-songs and a few drinks, whatever the result. They come from an old-fashioned country which breeds conscientious people, and I suppose it is typical of New Zealand cricket that some of their players over the years have refused to play cricket on Sundays. Bruce Murray and Vic Pollard were two such players in the seventies, and I can only respect their sincerity and try to think of another Test-playing country which selected men for whom playing Test matches was not their main purpose in life.

When Vic Pollard *did* play Test cricket, he was a gutsy, valuable batsman – particularly on the 1973 tour to England. Twice he scored hundreds, and each time he brought his side near to victory. At that time, New Zealand seemed to me to lack a killer instinct: it was almost as if they did not know how to win. In the first Test at Trent Bridge they were written off when they were facing nearly 500 to win. But Pollard and Bev Congdon got big hundreds, and at one stage they were just 70-odd short with half their wickets standing. Yet then they folded up. Later, at Lord's, they got a huge score, and England were really struggling when they batted for the second time. With eight wickets down, their keeper Ken Wadsworth dropped Geoff Arnold twice in successive balls, and England hung on for the draw. Then they beat the demoralized Kiwis by an innings in the final Test. I felt that with a more experienced team and a more ruthless captain, the tourists would have won at least one of those Tests. A man like Illingworth or Ian Chappell would have turned the screw at a vital moment, and the game would have been in the bag.

It must have been very frustrating for the Kiwis to see the realization of their dreams so tantalizingly close on that tour. Things did not quite go their way: Glenn Turner scored a thousand runs in May, yet he had gone off the boil by the time the Tests started; Richard Hadlee was still a raw fast bowler, despite his undoubted promise; Dick Collinge was probably too nice a guy to capitalize on his ability to make the ball rear up awkwardly. His left-arm seamers always troubled Boycott, but he lacked the aggression of a Lillee. I do not think they got the best out of Hedley Howarth on that tour; I may be biased because Hedley is a great friend of mine, but I think he was put on the scrap-heap too early. He was one of the best left-arm spinners around at that time: he was

94

BEV CONGDON

Bev Congdon was a player who maximized his resources and sold his wicket dearly. If all the Kiwis had shown Congdon's concentration and professionalism, the seventies would have been an even happier time for them. My kind of batsman: no frills, just a solid accumulator of runs. A big-innings man, he actually seemed to become a better player after he was made captain. Although he seemed an unimaginative leader, he made the best out of the assets at his disposal, and with a little more luck he might have grabbed an England victory several years before Wellington 1978.

A canny medium-pace bowler with the confidence to expect wickets, his main achievement for New Zealand was to instil greater confidence in their players. Congdon helped them lose that 'underdog' tag. A disciplined, friendly man, he kept himself very fit: at the age of forty, he was far from disgraced on his last tour of England.

always at you, would never give in, and was a brilliant fielder off his own bowling. The demands of a family fishing business, however, and a lack of support from his fielders speeded Hedley's exit from Test cricket. Bruce Taylor was another who never did himself justice at Test level. In his first Test he got a hundred and took five wickets, and it seemed New Zealand at last had a major all-rounder. He continued to be a devastating hitter of the ball on occasions, and he could swing the ball both ways and slip in a nasty bouncer. But he was never consistent enough with bat or ball, despite his obvious talent. That amateur spirit again – Bruce loved a laugh and joke on the field as well as in the bar, and there seems little room for that cheerful philosophy in modern Test cricket.

The Kiwis arrived in England with high hopes in 1978, and on the face of it they were justified in their optimism. The influence of county cricket had hardened up some of their key players, and they had achieved the psychological breakthrough against England a few months earlier at Wellington. But again they did not do themselves justice, and lost all three Tests. Yet twice they got themselves into good positions, only to lose the initiative. At the Oval, they made such an impressively solid start that Mike Brearley gave us a real roasting at lunch-time for our lethargy in the field. I could tell Mike was worried, but then the Kiwis gave it away. John Wright – a man I always have trouble bowling to, because he is such a good 'leaver' of a ball that is near his off-stump – hit a wide half-volley from me straight to mid-wicket after grafting away very impressively. Then Geoff Howarth pulled a long-hop from Ian Botham into square leg's hands when he was near his century. After that they collapsed – but in the second innings their best batsman, Geoff Howarth, was out for nought when he edged a slow, wide half-volley from me into his stumps. They folded up and we won easily.

At Lord's, they led us on the first innings by nearly fifty, a handy lead on an unreliable wicket, with Hadlee at last fit and bowling extremely well. On the Saturday night we were up against it as we went out to field for the New Zealand innings, but Mike Brearley paused at the dressing-room door and said to us: 'Look, if we get stuck in, we are capable of bowling this lot out for less than a hundred.' I don't know whether he was bluffing or being particularly perceptive, but Botham and I did just that – they got 67. Everything clicked for us, and it was just as well, because we could have been struggling if we had had to make 200. Our target was only just over 100, and even then Hadlee made us fret. He clean-bowled Boycott and Radley in successive balls with superb break-backs, and David Gower's coolness was important in seeing us home.

The luck did not go New Zealand's way, either. They were the victims of the rule that wickets must remain exposed to the elements once a ball has been bowled until the game is called off for the day. What happened at Trent Bridge was a repeat of the situation at Edgbaston in 1975, when the playing regulations handed the game to the Australians. On the Saturday of the Trent Bridge Test the light was appalling, and we could not believe it when the umpires went out to get the game started. As we trooped out, one of our team said: 'I hope we get just one ball at them before it starts to rain.' Well, we managed just two before the umpires ruled that the light was too bad. But the damage had been done, and the wicket was left uncovered. I came off behind the Kiwi captain, Mark Burgess, and I could see he was furious at the umpires for giving us the initiative for the sake of two balls. I could sympathize with him: he was very unlucky. We did not start play again till three o'clock; then we bowled them out by the end of the day, and won by an innings on the fourth day.

If New Zealand had an authentic foil to the excellent Hadlee, they would be a real force to be reckoned with. But on that 1978 tour, Hadlee was never consistently fit, Bracewell was too raw, Collinge over the top, and Cairns just a willing workhorse. Boock, a promising left-arm spinner, lacked experience, and their out-cricket was not very professional. They had not been able to replace Ken Wadsworth, their consistent wicket-keeper, who died so tragically of cancer at the age of twenty-nine; on this tour the job was shared by two of their batsmen – the promising Bruce Edgar and the jovial Jock Edwards, but neither was up to the job of keeper. Bob Taylor's immaculate displays for England served only to underline the difference, and the importance of having a class keeper. They dropped crucial catches as well: Boycott came back into the side at Trent Bridge after injury and, in a repeat of the Australian game from the previous year, he was missed at slip in the same place as McCosker dropped him. He had scored only two at the time and he went on to a hundred, at the same time laying the foundation for our victory.

They could have done with some of Boycott's attention to detail as well. He would not have made the mistakes of Robert Anderson and John Parker in their second innings at Trent Bridge: Anderson trying for a suicidal run to the brilliant Gower at mid-off; Parker slipping after

97

GLENN TURNER

Glenn Turner has been his country's most professional cricketer in more ways than one. He seemed to take a conscious decision to make money out of the game while dedicating himself to improving his standards. He realized he would be a faded photo on a wall within a few years; so, unlike previous talented Kiwi cricketers, he applied himself to his financial projects with the same single-minded devotion he shows in his batting.

When he first came to England, he was a very limited player; but he kept learning. The advent of one-day cricket meant that he had to accelerate the tempo of his innings. Like other master batsmen such as Gavaskar and Boycott, he worked out his limitations, then widened his horizons to become a great batsman. He has a very unusual grip, with the top hand twisted round the handle – but it works. A beautiful timer of the ball, he has often made me admire his ability to chip the ball over the inner cordon of fielders. That drives a bowler to distraction, and his length often suffers; then Turner picks off the runs. A thinking batsman, he paces his innings masterfully; and there cannot be many better to have around for a run chase.

Not the bravest of batsmen, he has been ruffled by several quick bouncers, including a few from myself. He sometimes steps away towards square leg and carves the quick stuff and, although it seems to work for him, that is a surprising lapse in a technique which is basically impeccable.

He has strong opinions, and his rows with the New Zealand Board have not helped his prospects of getting back into Test cricket. He is the only batsman to get a thousand runs in May since the War, so I suspect that the fact that he has never scored a Test century against England vexes him.

coming out to bat with no spikes in his boots after a shower of rain. In both cases they were run out, totally unnecessarily.

Gradually this amateur attitude to Test cricket is being broken down in New Zealand. The influence of English county cricket is spreading, both from the experience passed on by the Howarths and the Hadlees, but also in the increase in coaching visits from English pros like Clive Radley and Mike Selvey. I have had several offers to go out there and coach when my England touring days are over, but I doubt if I'll take the opportunity. It is a little too slow-moving out there for my taste, and cricket lacks the coaching facilities you would get in a place like South Africa.

I just hope that something can be done about the umpiring standard

in New Zealand. Quite frankly, in my opinion it is the worst in the world. I remember Derek Underwood simply giving up on L.B.W. appeals because they would turn down the plumbest ones you have ever seen. Then on the 1978 tour, the off-spinner Geoff Cope said at a team meeting: 'I'm sorry, lads, I'm no use to you in this country.' Geoff was right: every time the batsmen tried the sweep shot and missed, the L.B.W. appeal was turned down. In that same 1978 series, I remember vividly the first ball in the series: it was bowled by me, and John Wright nicked it to be caught by Bob Taylor diving in front of first slip. The umpire said 'not out' – it was astonishing. I think the best of their umpires is Fred Goodall, who has spent a recent season in English county cricket. I hope he learned a lot from the best umpires in the world, because New Zealand desperately needs the gospel to be spread. The trouble is that hardly any of them have played first-class cricket, and that lack of practical experience can be a disadvantage. There is very little money around in New Zealand cricket, and that is why the men who would be qualified to become umpires are not attracted to it. Although I would never condone the way the West Indies behaved on their last tour of New Zealand, there is no doubt that the defects of the umpires aggravated the situation.

I hope New Zealand continue their steady improvement in Test cricket during the next decade. Richard Hadlee has a few years left in him if he can get strike-bowling support at the other end; Edgar and Wright seem to have the right temperaments for the demands of Test cricket; while Geoff Howarth's batting does not seem to be affected by the strains of captaining his country. But they need a good wicket-keeper, and a solid middle-order batsman. Above all, they need Glenn Turner back in the fold. It is a terrific burden on a modest team when their best player is not available.

—6—

SOUTH AFRICA

I N purely cricketing terms, South Africa represents the biggest tragedy of the seventies. They played just four Tests at the start of the decade, and then the politicians took over. They have never got back into the Test fold, and I cannot really see much hope of that for some time. The balance of power on the I.C.C. would appear to be against them: I cannot see India, Pakistan and the West Indies countenancing their return until the structure of apartheid is dismantled.

All this ignores the fact that South Africa has gone a long way to putting its cricketing house in order in the last decade. When they left Test cricket in 1970, certain requirements for re-admission were laid down by the Cricket Council. Many good judges believe they were achieved long ago, and that cricket in the Republic is now run on non-racial lines. Unfortunately, politics and sport are now inextricably linked.

I visited South Africa three times in the seventies, and I was impressed with much of what I saw. Initially I went with typical left-wing views instilled in me by my upbringing. The D'Oliveira Affair was still fresh in my mind, and having played in the same England team as Basil, I could not help feeling sympathy for him. He desperately wanted to play cricket at Newlands in his home city of Cape Town, but that was always denied him, and I thought that dreadful. To me, the whole D'Oliveira Affair was a botch-up of monumental proportions; his original exclusion from the tour party in 1968 did not make sense after getting that hundred against Australia and the subsequent shifts and evasions on both sides seemed farcical. Only Basil came out of it all with his reputation improved and I, in common with most first-class cricketers, sided with him.

So I had the usual reflex action towards South Africa when I first went there in 1972 with the Derrick Robins team. I was staying with some charming people – the Murray family in Pretoria – and I remember standing in their beautiful home, telling them that if it had not been for the black man, they would not be sitting there, sipping a Scotch,

101

content with the world while black people sweated away outside. I didn't get on at all with the Afrikaaners, and could not see why the Dutch Reformed Church would want to preach apartheid. It was very disturbing to go into shops and see 'whites only' signs, or enter a railway station and see two sets of stairs which led to exactly the same place. But what I did not understand was that in South Africa not all the whites are under one philosophical flag, while the non-whites tend to stick to their own racial groups. I found the white, English-speaking people charming, with a social conscience about the need for change; yet the Afrikaaners were entrenched and dogmatic, despite having the same colour of skin. The non-whites are even more disparate: I recall one of the servants in the Murray's house telling me that if a member of another tribe came to work there, they would just kill each other. Many of the non-white sections of the South African community are poles apart in ideology; yet many well-intentioned critics of South Africa think that all non-whites are fighting together. I know it is the easiest thing in the world to say, but I really feel that you have to visit South Africa first and see how complex the apartheid question is before making the kind of declamatory statements I indulged in from the comfort of my left-wing, inexperienced stance.

I coached for the Northern Transvaal Cricket Union after the Robins tour ended in the 1972–3 season, and I played in the Currie Cup as well. I did not play all the time because they have a rule about limiting overseas players (compare England in the seventies!) and that much-travelled English fast bowler Allan Jones got the one place available. I played club cricket as well and enjoyed the away trips. The sides travelled vast distances to play, and I recall many happy hours spent in the roadside bars, whiling away the time before thinking about a game of cricket. The driving would get pretty hairy on those long journeys, and I particularly remember a time when our car did the Durban to Pretoria trip at a frantic eighty-five miles an hour when petrol rationing was at its height! We were stopped a couple of times by traffic police and, to this day, I still do not know how we got away with it. But the Currie Cup players I knew would often indulge in pranks like that on away trips – after all, it is an amateur sport there, these guys would take a week off work to play and the inclination to have a good time was very strong.

On the occasions when I have played in South Africa, I have been struck by how competitive it all is, at whatever level. This was particularly true about the Derrick Robins tour – we had players such as Frank

CRICKET AND POLITICS

Protest comes to cricket in 1970 when the 'Stop the 70 tour' campaign gathered full momentum. Lord's cricket ground was picketed regularly in the first half of the year, as efforts were increased to ban that summer's proposed tour by South Africa. Eventually the Home Secretary called off the tour because of the threat of civil disorder, and South Africa's isolation from Test cricket had begun.

MIKE PROCTER

Mike Procter leads off the South Africa side at Cape Town on the last day in Test cricket for his country. Procter had just taken six Australian wickets to leave Bill Lawry's 1970 touring team 4–0 losers in the series. A couple of months later, the balloon went up on South

African cricket when the 1970 tour to England was postponed because of a danger of public disorder – and since then, Procter and many other fine players have had to content themselves with substitutes for the real thing.

I cannot praise Mike Procter too much for the way he has battled against disappointment. With Gary Sobers past his best in the seventies, only Ian Botham could seriously challenge Procter's status as the world's greatest all-rounder – which made it doubly galling that he couldn't display his talents in Tests. A bad run of injuries in the mid-seventies would have finished lesser men, but Procter kept fighting away to get back to peak fitness.

A very talented batsman, he has been one of the sweetest strikers of the ball – not all that sound technically, but he can destroy you on his day. Particularly severe on medium-pacers and off-spinners, he is one of those men strong enough to mishit you for boundaries. As a fast bowler, he was devastating in his prime. An unorthodox action in which he seemed to deliver the ball fractionally early meant you were often surprised by the swing. He was very quick indeed in his day, but he needed a long run-up to generate pace. With a knack of getting hat-tricks with big, booming inswingers, he was an inspirational bowler. He is not a bad off-spinner, either – when he finally packs up quick bowling, he will still be in the game. He tosses the ball up a long way and gives the batsman a real mouthful if he won't take him on. Nor is he the most economical of off-spinners, but he can turn the ball.

A positive thinker, his comments have been an eye-opener for me when I have chatted to him about my own form, fitness, and future. It is a great tribute to Mike that he has gone through the whole decade with hardly a sniff of representative cricket (apart from Packer), yet he is still as keen as ever to do the county circuit with Gloucestershire and try his best with any side he represents. I have never heard him speak disparagingly about any of his players at Gloucestershire: despite his great all-round talent, he won't look down on somebody who is of limited ability. Socially he is excellent – he will talk to anybody in the bar, as long as they do not insult him with ill-informed monologues about apartheid. Other players of his eminence would creep away after the game and choose their own company; but Mike keeps his Gloucestershire side together, and will never be a strutting 'show pony'. He is a man who enjoys the game in England and its atmosphere, and Gloucestershire won't know what has hit them when he finally goes back to South Africa.

Sporting talent runs in the family: his brother and father played for Eastern Province; his wife was the number two women's tennis player in South Africa for a time; and, judging by the way Mike's son Gregg wields the bat, we should be seeing another Procter in first-class cricket in the near future.

Hayes, Clive Radley, John Lever, and Robin Jackman in our side, yet we were rolled over regularly. The same applied the following year when Robins took out players like Younis Ahmed, Brian Close, John Snow, Graham Roope and John Shepherd. The South Africans were very disappointed at being ostracized from Test cricket at that time. It was before disillusionment set in, and they were very keen to show they were still a force to be reckoned with.

This competitive streak comes from the schooling in South Africa. Sport among the whites is such an important thing out there that the will to win is instilled at a very early age. The climate is ideal for sport, and huge trophies are handed out at schools for things like being the best under-thirteen cricketer of the year. It is important to win things as an individual in a South African school. The schoolboys are disciplined as well: when I coached them at Pretoria High School, it was a rewarding experience. Only a couple of years earlier, I had been coaching boys of a similar age at Crystal Palace in London, and I was disappointed at their lack of discipline and concentration. I may not be the greatest coach in the world, but I felt those boys would have tried harder if they had really wanted to. No such problems in South Africa: the kids could not get enough of cricket. The facilities were un-believable – there were three full-sized cricket grounds at Pretoria High School, one of which was of county standard. There were grass and artificial nets, huge sight-screens, a brand new score-board, proper rollers and mowers and an overall air of pride in cricket. It was a tremendous start in life for any kid. The wickets are superb in South Africa as well: the school wickets are excellent, and the ones used in first-class cricket are just right for good batsmen and good bowlers.

Looking at the set-up in South Africa, it is clear why so many fine white cricketers keep rolling off the production line. Parental discipline is instilled in them right away, army training is compulsory, the facili-ties are out of this world, sport is worshipped out there, and there is every incentive to succeed. If only the talented non-white cricketers had the same opportunities, things would be even more satisfactory.

It must have been very galling for South Africa to be shut out from Test cricket just as they had pulled together their best side of all time. By 1970, the Pollock brothers, Ali Bacher, Eddie Barlow, Barry Richards, and Mike Procter were the basis of a high-quality side. They lacked a spin bowler, it is true; but judging by the way that Test sides became increasingly reliant on speed, they probably would not have needed much spin to get through the opposition. They had a blend of

VINTCENT VAN DER BIJL

Vintcent Van der Bijl has been the best bowler in the world *not* to play Test cricket in the seventies. I think he would have made an excellent third seamer behind Procter, Rice or Peter Pollock. As with Joel Garner, his enormous height gave him bounce on the slowest of wickets, while he bowled very near to the stumps, which gave him accuracy and the ability to bowl balls that deviated late off the pitch. A classical bowling action did not take too much out of him, so he could bowl long spells.

I met Vince in 1972 on the Robins Tour and I first saw his ability with the bat in one of our early games. Vince came in at number eleven for a South African XI and won the match with some huge hitting. He has remained a very useful batsman, and would have made a handy number nine in a Test side.

I never doubted that he would make the grade in county cricket, and I was delighted to see what an impact he had in his one season with Middlesex. A delightful man: he simply loves cricket and its players. Perhaps the fact that he has an excellent job in South Africa helps to keep him balanced about the game – but to me his ability to play professional cricket with an amateur spirit is a delight. I wish there were more like him in the game.

BARRY RICHARDS

Barry Richards was quite simply a marvellous batsman, not as destructive as Viv Richards, but a beautiful, stylish player. If Barry had enjoyed the regular incentive of Test cricket he would have made the lives of bowlers even more unbearable, while charming millions of spectators. When Barry set his mind to it, you had little or no chance of getting him out; he had so much time to play, it was heart-breaking if you were a bowler. He proved his brilliance all round the world – in English county cricket his technique was superb on difficult, damp pitches, while he did as well as anybody in World Series Cricket against Dennis Lillee.

My two outstanding memories of Barry do not concern the sheer beauty of his stroke play, but they disclose the less-publicized side of his batting. The first was at Durban on the Derrick Robins tour of 1973–4. The wicket was helping the bowlers, and John Snow was in superb form. Snow was really trying, and for six overs in a row Barry played the same shot – a defensive one off the back foot. Barry could not get him off the square, but it was a masterpiece of defensive batting. At lunch, he showed me his right hand. It was badly bruised from the jarring shock of the ball during those punishing overs. It had been an ordeal against a great fast bowler – but Barry had won.

Then there was the time when we met him in Australia. Barry was in the nets, and some blokes were throwing the ball at him from about fifteen yards. There was Barry practising his off-drives with the precision of a Boycott, getting the same part of the bat to the ball all the time and guiding it through various angles. He did this for at least half an hour, and I couldn't but reflect how interesting it was to watch a master batsman perfecting one particular shot while lesser mortals of Test standard were shufflling around in the nets trying to sort out some semblance of a batting technique.

Although Barry always gave the air of being casual and cool, he practised a fair amount. And when he was a youngster in South Africa, the day was not long enough for him in the nets. What a tragedy that events beyond his control stopped him from developing his talents even further. I always got on very well with Barry, but it must be said that money occupied too much of his mind. I don't blame him for signing for Packer, but I think he let Hampshire down in his last few months with them. He did not do the image of South African cricketers any good by clearing off in mid-season just after picking up his benefit.

fast-scoring batsmen (Graeme Pollock, Barry Richards, and Mike Procter) with solidity (Eddie Barlow, Ali Bacher, 'Tiger' Lance), a fine wicket-keeper/batsman (Denis Lindsay) and aggressive fast bowling (Peter Pollock and Procter). They caught everything in that series against the Australians in 1970, and by the end of the tour Bill Lawry's side were totally demoralized. With West Indies in decline at that time, with England's limited resources being held together only by a great captain, Ray Illingworth, and the other Test countries still emerging from the shadows of being the whipping-boys from previous decades, there is no doubt in my mind that South Africa were the real world champions in 1970.

It is exciting but also frustrating to sit down and contemplate what kind of a side South Africa would have been able to put out in later years. In addition to the players already mentioned, there are Clive Rice, Vintcent Van der Bijl, Garth le Roux, Peter Kirsten, Lee Irvine, Denys Hobson (their one world-class spinner of the decade, a fact Kerry Packer realized), and Chris Wilkins. English county cricket represents a great breeding-ground for South Africans to professional-ize their talents; I feel there have been too many overseas players allowed into county cricket, but there is no doubt that the exciting skills of the South Africans have entertained greatly. And they keep coming along: of the younger breed, Hampshire's Chris Smith and Warwick-shire's Anton Ferreira should develop into top-class players, while Allan Lamb of Northamptonshire could easily become the batsman of the eighties. When you bowl at a guy like Allan Lamb, you realize how lucky he has been to learn his batting on superb wickets. Quite apart from his glittering natural talent, he has the confidence, the knack of selecting the right line and playing the right shot to the particular delivery that invariably comes from growing up on hard, true wickets.

Another thing I have admired about the South Africans is the way they have thrown themselves into county cricket. Men like Barlow, Rice and Procter have helped revitalize their counties; they haven't stood on the sidelines, content to pick up a good contract and just do their stuff. Their example has helped many English players become better cricketers. I suppose their enthusiasm for the English game stems from the fact that they don't play cricket full-time back home; it is still an amateur sport out there, although improved sponsorship is making it a more rewarding career. A man such as Mike Procter has to secure his own future away from the cricket field in South Africa: there is not enough cricket to play, so he has to develop a business career. So when he and the other South Africans come back to English county cricket every year, they are happy to buckle down to the daily grind, because it is a change from the set-up back home.

Although I admire immensely the way a typical South African cricketer will give his all on the field and then be the first to buy you a drink in the bar, I do not like his attitude to umpires. In this respect, the South Africans are almost as bad as the Australians – Tony Greig was typical of the way the Springboks played their cricket: hard and un-yielding, and do not try to help out the umpire. Greig, Barlow, & Co. would always assume that the breaks would go against them on other occasions, so they saw no reason why they should look a gift horse in the mouth when an umpire made a bad decision in their favour. I think the umpiring in South Africa is poor, and its effects have led to an increase in gamesmanship and 'sledging' in the Currie Cup, where the rivalry between the sides is intense because the players have nothing higher to aim for through being denied a Test platform. Not enough retired first-class cricketers go into umpiring in South Africa, because it is a wealthy country with plenty of opportunities for advancement – and umpiring is not well paid there, nor particularly rewarding because there is no incentive to aim towards Test standard. Having said that, one wonders if they really would be any better.

The quality of umpiring over there is best summed up by the time when Ian Chappell, of all people, was outwitted in a Johannesburg Test. Chappell edged the ball which apparently bounced about two feet in front of 'Tiger' Lance at second slip. Chappell asked him if he had caught it and when that was confirmed, he walked off to the pavilion. Chappell had his back to the incident, so he just had to rely on Lance's word; anyway, when he got back into the Aussie dressing-room, he was told that 'Tiger' had caught the ball on the bounce. Afterwards, over a beer, Chappell challenged 'Tiger' about saying that he had caught it – only to get the devastating reply that he hadn't asked him whether it had bounced first! That is a story that amuses many South Africans, I know – not just because Chappell was outsmarted, but because they think it is fair enough to fool the umpire as well. They tend to forget that without good umpiring, the game just becomes a shambles, and that we should try to help them. But that may be becoming an idealistic and outdated attitude, I am afraid.

Apart from lapses into gamesmanship, I have liked most of the South African cricketers I have come across. They do not have the chip on the shoulder many Australians have, and I think it is tremendous that they

111

EDDIE BARLOW

Eddie Barlow epitomized South African cricket. He would give you nothing at all on the field, and would do the umpires no favours either – yet at the end of the day, he would be great company. One of the greatest triers I have ever known, his concentration on the field was unbelievable: batting, bowling, fielding, or captaining, you got precious little chat out of Eddie.

In the Rest of the World series against England in 1970, he showed his value to the side by grafting away to get two hundreds, even though his technique was always too loose for English wickets, where the ball seams around a lot. He took valuable wickets as well with unpredictable bowling – like Botham, he had the knack of getting wickets with terrible deliveries; but, in fairness to him, he always attacked and gave the batsmen something to hit. As a slip fielder, Eddie was one of the best around.

He made a very fine captain with the knack of transforming mediocre players into good performers. He turned both Western Province and Derbyshire upside down; the difference in the Derbyshire side was particularly remarkable. Bob Taylor often told me how interesting it was to play under Barlow: he would regularly give them the day off and tell them to stay away from the ground, so that they would arrive the next day fresh and ready for cricket. But woe betide any player who did not toe the line, particularly in fitness terms! At Derbyshire, I gather he got rid of two England players, Phil Sharpe and Alan Ward, because they did not think much of the training schedules Eddie had left them to fulfil during the English winter. And Mike Hendrick has a lot to be grateful for to Eddie because, until he arrived at Derby, Hendrick was very down with the endless visits he had to make to the physiotherapist's table. But Eddie sorted out Mike's depression and his fitness problems alike, and the transformation was England's gain.

He is an immensely likeable man, and I am not surprised he has gone into politics. He is a serious-minded individual with a strong social conscience, who has done a lot for the progress towards non-racial cricket in his country.

have battled away to maintain their cricketing standards, even though they could not aspire to Test cricket. It must have been disappointing for such men as Mike Procter to see how much money could be made out of modern Test cricket by players not fit enough to tie their boots – all the while building up false hopes each time a citadel of segregated sport toppled in South Africa. Those inconclusive statements from the I.C.C. conference every July must have depressed Richards, Pollock, &

Co. deeply; at last the cricketing house seemed to have been put in order, yet the only encouragement they would get from the game's rulers was a qualified pat on the back for making gradual progress. It is true that county cricket has been a substitute for many of them – and a creative challenge to Barlow, Procter, and Rice as they have successfully transformed struggling sides – but as someone hooked on Test cricket, I can just imagine the frustration that I would feel. No wonder

113

they signed like a shot for Kerry Packer; for Barry Richards, one of the greatest batsmen of his age, it must have been a wonderful incentive.

If only rugby could make the same sort of strides as cricket towards non-racial sport in South Africa. After all, cricket is really the English-speaking white man's game, while rugby is the god for the Afrikaaner. Although the Springbok rugby side has faced isolation, it has still been able to play a fair amount of internationals. Indeed the visit of the British Lions to South Africa in 1980 unwittingly gave a further cloak of respectability to the status quo in the Republic. I cannot see rugby putting its house in order in the same way as cricket over there; can you imagine any of the top Springbok players doing what Procter, Richards, Barlow, and all the other stars did at Newlands in 1971, when they staged a walk-off in a match and publicly declared their opposition to the Government's sports policy? That took a lot of guts, and it definitely accelerated progress towards a non-racial cricket programme. Yet it did not bring South Africa back into Test cricket, despite some strange standards set by other member countries of the I.C.C. After all, Australia only allows non-whites from other countries to settle there in exceptional circumstances while, on my travels to the West Indies, I have experienced anti-white treatment in places like Guyana and Jamaica that is as strong as anything expressed by a hard-nosed Afrikaaner. But nobody ever suggests that the West Indies or Australia should be banned from Test cricket!

The Robin Jackman affair in 1981 only underlined the depth of hostility towards South Africa from certain parts of the West Indies. In the short term, the fuss over Robin's South African connections threatened the England tour and focused attention on some hypocritical standards – but, in the long run, I fear the Jackman Affair crystallized the West Indian antipathy towards any planned re-admission of South Africa to Test cricket. The day of re-entry seems further away than 'ever.

—7—

WEST INDIES

TEST cricket in the seventies became more of a serious matter for the West Indies. Not that I have ever swallowed the myth that West Indian cricketers are a fun-loving, calypso-singing lot; in the latter half of the decade, they became a hard, unrelenting outfit who had worked out the way to play successful Test cricket. They seemed to get over-professional in the zeal to win, not least of all because Kerry Packer had given the comparatively poor West Indians a glimpse of untold riches.

Despite the high quality on display, Tests against the West Indies were not pleasant affairs in my time. I sensed an undercurrent of bad feeling on the field of play and, afterwards, there was little social fraternizing between England and West Indies. The lack of artificial social functions did not distress me too much, but I was more concerned that the colour issue possibly clouded relationships. In county cricket, a West Indian is fine as he integrates smoothly into the harmony of a multi-racial side, but once a West Indian team steps on to the field for his country, some of them seem to change character. I noticed that particularly on my first England tour of the West Indies in 1974; in their side were Lance Gibbs, Rohan Kanhai, Deryck Murray and Alvin Kallicharran, who were Warwickshire team-mates of Dennis

ENGLAND v. THE WEST INDIES				
Season	Tests	Won by England	Won by West Indies	Drawn
1973	3	0	2	1
1973–4	5	1	1	3
1976	5	0	3	2

115

DERYCK MURRAY

Deryck Murray was a very influential man in the West Indies Test history of the past decade – and not just because he always seemed to be behind the stumps. His university background and family business connections equipped him ideally for the task of chief negotiator with Kerry Packer on behalf of the West Indian players. Those with lesser intellects would bring their contracts and financial problems to Deryck, and he would sort them out. For many of them, the money was a real crock of gold, because their Board never had much cash to go round. So his business acumen was very valuable.

I played with him at Warwickshire for a number of years, but I could never get all that close to him. When we went out to play the West Indies, Deryck did not exactly put out the welcome mat for his team-mates, Amiss, Jameson and myself. He kept himself very fit over the years, and his temperament was excellent. A great man in a crisis, he sold his wicket dearly, but he was clearly shell-shocked by the barrage of speed in World Series Cricket.

His wicket-keeping could vary from the spectacularly good to the embarrassingly bad. He was not very good at standing up to the spinners, but then I suppose no modern keeper got better practice at standing back than Deryck Murray.

Amiss, John Jameson and myself who were on the tour. Seldom did the four West Indians appear very friendly to us, a fact I found remarkable, considering we had shared so many ups and downs in English county cricket. I suspect Rohan had a lot to do with that, because he badly wanted to beat us; but I cannot believe that a policy of friendliness towards county team-mates dilutes the will to win at Test level. Thank heaven Ian Botham and Viv Richards have shown enough common sense to avoid such a situation.

Test cricket the West Indian way had become an easy game to play by the end of the seventies – provided you had the means at your disposal. Clive Lloyd had them in abundance: a succession of fast-scoring batsmen who would give him enough time to bowl out the opposition twice, plus a production line of fast bowlers who monopolized the West Indies out-cricket. Running their team in the field became as regimented as crop rotation: Lloyd would perm four fast bowlers from an impressive selection and simply wheel them up at selected stages. Because they bowled so quickly, only the very best batsmen could prosper – and if at any rare stage the batsmen got on top, Lloyd could always slow down the over rate if he wanted. The longer it takes to bowl an over, the fewer deliveries the batsmen have to hit, and the greater the chance that they get frustrated and lose their wickets in an effort to boost the scoring. So Clive Lloyd did not have to be an inspirational leader: secure in the knowledge that the I.C.C. would merely 'tut tut' about slow over rates in the seventies and not introduce compulsory rates, Lloyd just had to work out when to go on the defensive. At the same time, Test captains such as Mike Brearley, Bobby Simpson and Graham Yallop were trying to achieve things with inferior talent at their disposal. Clive Lloyd's tactics towards the West Indies out-cricket in my view produced a boring formula that made his team the world champions.

The West Indies tour of Australia in 1975–6 was the tactical water-shed for Lloyd's team. They arrived there as World Cup holders, with morale high and a determination to see off Lillee and Thomson with far more aggressive methods than stodgy old England had shown the previous year. They met disaster. Only one Test went beyond the fourth day, and the West Indies were slaughtered 5–1. They simply fell apart: they allowed controversial umpiring decisions to upset them; the Australians' occasionally abusive tactics on the field distracted them; and Lillee and Thomson took over fifty wickets as batsman after batsman perished to the hook shot.

117

CLIVE LLOYD

Clive Lloyd has been a father-figure to many West Indian players. He grew up in the shadow of Kanhai and Sobers, but established himself as a fine Test batsman with tremendous powers of hitting. He looks dodgy at the start of his innings, but he is the hardest hitter I have known.

When the Packer offer came along, Lloyd was more honest than others when he admitted it was just too good to turn down. Once the captain had indicated his support for World Series Cricket, the other players followed suit. He had earned the respect of his team by the way he had come back from that dreadful tour of Australia, where his captaincy was unimpressive – so inevitably his players would want to stick with him.

In my opinion he has never been a great captain, by any stretch of the imagination. I have never been able to understand why Joel Garner has to wait so long before he gets to bowl. Roberts, Holding & Co. wheel away getting the shine off the ball while Garner kicks his heels; but then he comes on and bowls superbly. Garner bowls enough unplayable deliveries when the ball is eighty overs old to make me wonder what he would do if he was given the new ball after six or seven overs. Then the faster bowlers could fire away at the other end, while Garner enjoyed himself with the bright, shiny cherry.

Lloyd has had it easier than most Test captains, because his tactics have been clearly thought out and he sticks to them. After all, they are successful – but that is more to do with the talent at his disposal than any leadership qualities. He is also too passive in the field, in my opinion, and he allows certain things to go on that should never be tolerated – Old Trafford 1976 and Dunedin 1980, to name but two.

Judging by past West Indian selectorial panics, Clive Lloyd seemed lucky to keep the captaincy after that tour. He had learned a few lessons from it. In that series the West Indies bowled more balls per hour than the Australians – on average they sent 93 balls an hour. Admittedly Lance Gibbs bowled a fair number of off-breaks, but the fact remained that their over rate was perfectly respectable. It had rebounded in their face, because it gave the Aussies more balls to hit against the demoralized West Indian fielders. After that series the West Indies hardly bothered with spin. Padmore, Parry, Jumadeen and Inshan Ali made spasmodic Test appearances, but did not exactly get overbowled, and in the process the West Indian over rate had slumped to just over 70 balls an hour by 1980. They had learned from the Chappell brothers – and possibly from England in previous decades – how to stop the opposition from running away with the match on a batsman's wicket –

simply give them as few balls as possible to play.

There were other significant sequels to that series in Australia – Viv Richards emerged as one of the few West Indian batsmen not to be dominated by Lillee and Thomson, and from there he proceeded to become the finest batsman in the world. After some controversial umpiring decisions, the West Indies seemed to follow the lead of the Australians : don't walk even when you believe you are out, appeal as often as possible because the law of averages will be on your side, and don't hesitate to intimidate batsmen with short-pitched fast bowling if the umpires do not prevent it. A few months later, Brian Close and John Edrich were on the receiving end at Old Trafford of the most terrifying, sustained intimidation I have ever seen. The wicket had suffered in the drought of 1976 and it was just one long series of corrugated strips, so that if the ball struck one of them, it would rear up

119

off a length and whizz past the batsman's nose. Holding, Roberts and Daniel bowled bouncer after bouncer on the Saturday night and they got away with it while Edrich and Close gave the bravest display of batting imaginable. To me, it was a graphic illustration of the way the West Indies had toughened up after the traumas of Australia.

I suppose the West Indian temperament is suited to that style of bowling. They seem to churn out fast bowlers every year, and in a place like Barbados there must be at least fifteen quickies who either play county cricket or have the ability to do so. It seems ingrained in the West Indian psyche that it is good to see a batsman hopping around and ducking under spectacularly fast bowling, even though it sometimes does not get wickets. A man like Joel Garner is more deadly at the highest level, because he varies his length and bowls devastating yorkers almost at will – but he is a rarity, because the West Indian likes to see the ball pitched short and fly around the batsman's ears.

One of the most influential factors in the rise to eminence of West Indies Test cricket has been the English county scene. Because we

THE SLOW OVER RATE

One of the tactics that makes the West Indies less than endearing is the ridiculous time they take to bowl their overs. To me, it is a deliberate tactic designed to slow down the game and to stop the opposition getting much opportunity to launch an offensive. No matter how fast you are capable of scoring, there is little hope of beating the West Indies if you do not see too many deliveries. Clive Lloyd would simply rotate his four pace bowlers throughout the day, giving them three spells of about six overs each. The public would be cheated out of about an hour's play by the dawdling back to the mark while the West Indies would steadfastly maintain that the spectators were happy because they came to see great fast bowlers.

Now my run-up is not exactly short, and I do accept the need for a long run to generate rhythm – but in county cricket, we are taught to get back to the mark as quickly as possible; otherwise we are fined for a slow over rate. In English cricket, an acceptable rate is just over 19 an hour; yet the West Indians – many of whom have experience of county cricket – never seem to get above 13 or 14 an hour.

England tried to do something about over rates in 1980 when they asked the International Cricket Conference to insist on a minimum of $16\frac{1}{4}$ overs per hour in Tests, failing which fines would be levied. This was thrown out, so the West Indies continue to exploit the situation while telling us that they are giving the public what they want.

IAN CHAPPELL TEACHES THE WEST INDIES A LESSON

This is the moment when the West Indies came face to face with the
stark realities of Test cricket in the seventies. It's Sydney in 1976, and
Clive Lloyd's side are 2–1 down in the series and trying desperately
for a breakthrough. Ian Chappell plays at his first ball from Michael
Holding, and all the close fielders are convinced he has edged it to the
wicket-keeper, Deryck Murray. Chappell, as usual, stands his
ground, and umpire Reg Ledwidge gives him 'not out'. That sparked
off an amazing performance from Holding: he cried, gesticulated, and
sat down for five minutes, refusing to bowl. Lance Gibbs and Clive
Lloyd had to plead with him to resume the over. Eventually Chappell
was out, caught Murray, bowled Holding, ironically enough. He had
only scored four, but the psychological damage to the West Indies
was done. Greg Chappell came in, was dropped when he had scored
only eleven, and went on to make 182 not out as the West Indies were
distracted and moaned about the umpiring. They allowed their concentration to lapse completely: they lost the Test and ended up 5–1
losers of the series.

After that series, the West Indian became a meaner Test cricketer.
They did no favours to the umpires or the opposition. Ian Chappell
had gained some illustrious converts to his philosophy of how Test
cricket should be played.

122

obligingly opened our doors from 1968 onwards to overseas players, English county cricket has proved to be a great training ground for other Test teams. I think it is the most consistently demanding brand of cricket in the world (apart from Tests themselves), and anyone who prospers in county cricket has a good chance of going one step higher. That is a point consistently pushed home by Alec Bedser, England's chairman of selectors. After we had been hammered at home by the West Indies, Alec pointed out that we could not expect a young English batsman such as Frank Hayes to develop into a consistent Test player when a bloke like Clive Lloyd was batting ahead of him at Lancashire. Many derided Alec at that time; but he was not making shallow excuses for England being outclassed, he was stating the facts of life. The West Indian side that beat England by an innings and plenty at Lord's in 1973 was entirely made up of players who had honed their skills in English county cricket – apart from Maurice Foster. In the previous Test at Edgbaston all eleven had played county cricket. Since then the only influential West Indian cricketer who has not played county cricket has been Michael Holding.

That West Indian side recovered some of its self-respect after a bad series against us in 1969. With Gary Sobers in decline they lacked inspiration, and they had lost series to India and Australia at home. In Rohan Kanhai they picked the right man to captain them on that England tour. He was easily their best captain I have known: he was shrewd, vastly experienced, and would attack on most occasions. I once saw him score an astonishing hundred at Coventry, out of 120 on a dreadful wicket. A player who could drop anchor for the good of the side, he made a major contribution to their first World Cup win by keeping one end secure, while Clive Lloyd blazed away to get his match-winning hundred in the final. Kanhai's rivalry with Gary Sobers often amused other players. They were both superb performers with a lot of pride and self-respect, and each would try to outdo the other. In the Lord's Test in 1973, Kanhai stole a trick on Gary: Rohan had played a beautiful innings of 157 when Gary came in with the score about 300 for 4, a great sight for any toiling fast bowler. He proceeded to smash us around the place, only stopping to retire to the pavilion to answer the call of nature. Anyway, he came back and played typically, even though he was virtually on one knee by that time. He got to 150 and must have fancied passing Rohan's score but, just as I was about to take the third new ball, Rohan declared!

Rohan and Gary did not often have long partnerships together,

123

partly because they kept vying with each other, but they were a tremendous pair of batsmen. Gary was limping around painfully for most of that season, and I think he regretted signing on for Nottinghamshire in 1968. The money was good, and after all Gary was never the greatest at holding on to his cash; but there was little atmosphere at Trent Bridge, and they had little chance of winning a trophy. He was always a great bloke to play against: on the first morning of the match he would come into the opposition dressing-room and say: 'Hello, lads, everything OK with you? How's it been this season?' He loved a laugh and a bet on the horses. I was very sad when one day he told me: 'I feel fine, Bob, but as soon as I get to the ground the energy just drains away from me.' After all, he played cricket non-stop all round the world for about fifteen years, and that takes its toll of even a genius like Gary. Even in the seventies, when he was past his prime, he was still a great batsman who gave the ball a terrific crack. I remember the first time I bowled at him. It was in 1969: I had taken the first four Nottinghamshire wickets very cheaply, and I fancied myself to get the great Sobers as well. My first ball to him bounced about two yards in front of Gary, and then went straight back over my head and clattered against the sight-screen!

A fabulous cricketer, Gary was the best new-ball bowler I have ever seen, with a glorious action that did not require a long run-up. I am glad to have played against the greatest all-rounder ever, even though he was no longer at his best. I wonder what this genial man would have made of the behaviour of some of the West Indies players in later years. For Gary was always a chivalrous cricketer, and a man incapable of even pretending to be grim and remorseless on the field. To him, cricket was only a game.

There were some other talented cricketers in that 1973 West Indian side as well. Bernard Julien played a remarkable attacking innings in the Lord's Test when we were on our knees, and I recall thinking what a lovely clean hitter he was. He was a fine left-arm seamer as well, who could bowl surprise bouncers, but he got stuck with the 'new Sobers' tag, and never did himself justice. In county cricket, Kent batted him too far down the order, and he lacked application for the day-to-day grind of county cricket. He was not a great success with W.S.C., either. Another man on that tour with bags of natural talent was Keith Boyce: he was a gloriously free hitter of the 'hit-or-miss' variety, who bowled fast, troubling Boycott with the bouncer. There were few better outfielders in the seventies than Keith Boyce – fast to the ball with an astonishingly strong throw that had Deryck Murray leaping around all over the place behind the stumps.

Vanburn Holder was doing a lot of the seam-bowling donkey-work around this time for the West Indies. He slogged around India twice for them, and that is no picnic for any bowler. Vanburn bowled quite quickly at times, and he could do a lot with the ball as well.

So the West Indies had bags of talent in their side, but often it was not properly used. An example of this was our next series against them, in the West Indies. We were always fighting them off over there: yet we sneaked a win in the last Test which levelled the series and which, considering the respective merits of the two sides, was ridiculous. That tour was a disastrous one for England, because we just papered over the cracks; they gaped open again the following year in Australia. It was Mike Denness's first tour as England captain, and his lucky escape with a draw gave him a breathing-space that I do not think he really deserved. Along with most of the England team, I did not think Ray Illingworth deserved to be sacked after the West Indies thrashed us at Lord's. True, he was forty-one, but he was still worth his place in the side, and remained a great captain.

Mike Denness was not selected for England in the summer, so it was difficult enough for him in playing terms on that tour, quite apart from learning the ropes of Test captaincy. Unfortunately Mike just didn't seem to inspire confidence, and he found it difficult to get through to the players. Things just drifted along on and off the field, and I became very disenchanted both with my own form and with the shape of our side. It is true that at this stage of my career I was still very immature and did not have the right attitude to training, but I felt the captain should have taken a more positive lead when things started going wrong. After the first Test defeat he called a team meeting in which the bowlers' tactics were roundly criticized, but there was to be no mention of the way our batsmen had thrown away the match. So I piped up: 'What about the batting?' and Mike seemed rather embarrassed by it all. It was even worse in a meeting before the Barbados Test: Mike told us that Arnold, Old, and me would be the seam bowlers and Geoff Arnold asked, 'Who's going to have the new ball?'

'Old and Willis,' replied Mike.

I chipped in again and said that Geoff Arnold was the best new-ball bowler in the world, and Mike agreed. Now it may have been wrong of me to put pressure on the captain, but I felt Mike should have been firmer.

ALVIN KALLICHARRAN

Alvin Kallicharran, seen here with Viv Richards. His Test record shines throughout the seventies, even if fast bowling eventually wore him down a little. A nimble, quick-footed left-hander, he was at his best against England in 1973–4, when we played eight Tests in the space of nine months. Lillee and Thomson sorted him out in 1975–6, but he still retained the ability to score heavily and attractively.

A lot of people tell me I bowl very well at Alvin, but I have never swallowed that one. True, I know his faults quite well because we have played many years together at Warwickshire, and it is also true that my inslant action gets the left-hander in trouble just outside the off-stump. However, Alvin has taken a lot of runs off me, and in 1974 I never looked like getting him out.

Alvin got out of his depth when he signed for Kerry Packer, and he soon regretted it. He was pulled by both sides at Warwickshire: by Dennis Amiss, who had already signed for World Series Cricket; and by our captain, David Brown, who was very anti-Packer. Alvin did not realize that he might face a ban from county cricket if he played for W.S.C., and without a contract with Warwickshire, he would not have been able to stay in Britain. He was in the process of establishing Birmingham as his home, and going back to Guyana was a prospect that did not appeal to him. So he pulled out of W.S.C., and his reward was the West Indies captaincy. He did well with virtually a Third XI on the tour to India.

Morale was bad right from the start of the tour, and it really slumped when we were put in to bat on a damp wicket at Port of Spain. Consequently we lost the first Test by a wide margin. What annoyed the bowlers so much was the batting collapse in the second innings which lost the match. Boycott and Amiss had put on over 200 for the first wicket, and at one stage we were 328 for 1. Then Mike Denness was run out from the boundary's edge by Alvin Kallicharran as he was going for a third run – and we folded up and did not even get to 400. Game, set and match to the West Indies.

A lot of fuss was made about the incident when Tony Greig ran out Alvin Kallicharran at close of play on the second day, but to be honest, the headlines made the affair seem more sinister than it was. I was fielding backward point at the time. Derek Underwood bowled the last ball, which Greig fielded. Alvin walked off, followed by half the England players, and then the stumps were thrown down. The umpire had not called 'time'; so, legally, Greig was in the right. I agree it seemed an inflammatory thing to do, but it was done in the heat of the moment at the end of a long day where England had been utterly dominated – and something just snapped. It was all smoothed over afterwards, and Alvin was reinstated. That incident did not do Tony Greig any good at all in the eyes of Lord's; in the cold light of the day, I suppose he deserved the criticism.

At least he was one of the few England players to enhance his reputation on that tour. Another was Dennis Amiss, who made a lot of runs – usually in the second innings when the wicket had got flat. His powers of concentration were immense; this was particularly evident at Kingston, where he saved the game for us with 262 not out. Dennis got in the right frame of mind at the start of the tour when he and Boycott put on a big stand against the President's Eleven, and then came the 200 partnership in the first Test. I shudder to think what we would have done without Boycott and Amiss.

Pretty soon, our tactics in the Tests became more and more negative. We were never really within shouting distance of victory until the last Test. Before then, we seemed to be trying just to avoid defeat and to frustrate their talented side. Keith Fletcher and Alan Knott held them up at Bridgetown in the third Test, and the rain prevented a positive result at Georgetown. So to the final one, and a remarkable performance by the West Indies. They gave us the match on a plate. Although the wicket was turning, they needed only just over 200 to win; yet when Clive Lloyd stupidly ran out Roy Fredericks, their great

127

players just panicked. Tony Greig's extra height gave him enough bounce for his off-spinners to let him take thirteen wickets in the match.

The supreme irony of that England victory was that the two men who coveted the captaincy kept Mike Denness in the job for another year. Tony Greig and Geoff Boycott made no secret of the fact that they didn't seem to rate Denness; yet because they were both big-occasion players, they would never let personal considerations get in their way. Boycott batted beautifully in that last Test and narrowly missed two hundreds in the match, while Greig's bowling was decisive. Having won the Test, Mike Denness could not be sacked, could he? He came back to England as the captain who'd drawn a series in the West Indies – on the face of it, no mean achievement – so, unless he was a major disaster in the games against India and Pakistan, he was a certainty to lead the team in Australia. That was how it turned out.

That 1974 series proved to be the end of the road for a lot of the West Indies players. They could not believe that we had come from behind, and although we all knew that our win was ill-deserved, they nevertheless realized that wholesale changes for the future were needed. Kanhai and Sobers never played Test cricket again, and among others Gibbs, Julien and Boyce faded from the scene. Only Lloyd, Murray, Kallicharran, and Fredericks remained to form the nucleus of their strong side of 1976. Lawrence Rowe established himself against Denness's team, and he looked a very fine player. But Rowe must be one of the great enigmas in cricket: people kept saying he was going to be another George Headley, yet he never seemed completely fit. He failed in county cricket, even though he had everything a great batsman needs. He took three hundreds off us on Mike Denness's tour, including a triple century in the Barbados Test that was a superb piece of clean hitting. I remember him hitting me right out of the ground as I followed instructions to keep bouncing him – and I also remember he was run out on 199 by a good six inches. The crowd would have rioted if he had been give out just one run short of his double hundred. I was amazed to get an L.B.W. decision against him in the second Test in front of his home crowd. Mind you, he had scored a hundred by then! Perhaps it was a compensation for the previous game we had played against Jamaica, when Bob Taylor caught Rowe off Geoff Arnold with the first ball of the match. It was the loudest snick I have ever heard; but Rowe stayed, went on to get a hundred, and then took three more off us in the Tests.

That Test in which Rowe got his triple hundred was significant in

ANDY ROBERTS

I think Andy Roberts has been the most complete fast bowler of the seventies, apart from Dennis Lillee. Off a shortish run, he would bustle in and bowl deceptively slow deliveries that would get you playing too early, and then he would slip in a vicious bouncer. He can bowl two types of bouncer: the slowish, tennis-ball one that you can see all the way and the one that skids through and follows you. In his first season in county cricket, he caught several experienced players with the quick bouncer, including Colin Cowdrey who was knocked out and fell on to his wicket.

His explosive start in county cricket is typical of the way West Indian fast bowlers burst on the scene. He had only played a handful of matches in the Shell Shield yet, in his first season, he was the most devastating bowler in England.

Cold and unemotional both on and off the field, he never gets flustered if a decision goes against him. He does not rubbish the umpire; he will take it out on the batsmen instead. Very accurate, his striking rate is most impressive. With his excellent temperament for Test cricket, he has made himself into a very useful batsman, able to block and give the strike to a class player or, if necessary, to slog a few himself.

129

another way for the future of West Indies Test cricket: it marked the début of Andy Roberts. He was raw, and he only took three wickets in the Test, after which he was dropped. He looked distinctly sharp, and bowled far better than his figures suggested. By that time he had qualified for Hampshire, and was set to make his championship début later that year. He was an instant success, and he has remained the most consistently aggressive West Indian bowler since.

If I have one vivid memory from that unhappy tour, it must be the atmosphere in the ground at Port of Spain when we won the last Test. Just a couple of months previously the whole ground had been alive and humming as we were thrashed in the first Test. The West Indian players as well as the crowd were dancing around, shaking their cans with stones inside, making a fearful row. It was like being at a disco; they were beside themselves with joy. On the last day of the final Test there was nothing but eerie silence. Hardly anybody was there to see the West Indies beaten, and the contrast neatly summed up the volatile nature of Caribbean cricket.

They certainly did not lack volatile support in 1976 when they beat us 3–0 in England. The long, hot summer suited their players, while their supporters flocked to see them. It felt as if we were playing in the West Indies, judging by the heat and the exuberant support for their team. They had one of the best post-war touring sides to England. In purist terms the balance was still wrong, because their spinners Padmore and Jumadeen only played in one Test each; but their fast bowlers were so devastating that they did not really need moderate spin bowling. The batting was strong on paper, with Greenidge and Richards having established themselves in the previous couple of years, and their experience of English conditions was crucial. Richards was simply Richards, the man around whom the side has revolved since 1976. Roy Fredericks was still a very fine player – neat, whippy with a taste for the hook shot – and there were also Lloyd, Kallicharran and Rowe.

If I had to look at weaknesses in that team, I would say that none of their specialist batsmen was a good enough bowler (say to the standard of Eddie Barlow), so that everything rested on their four-pronged speed attack. Their batting just died after Deryck Murray at number seven. Holding, Roberts, Holder, and Daniel were not a lasting problem for the bowlers, even though Holder was often good for a few, and Roberts later became a very useful tail-ender. That imbalance in their batting order meant that we always thought we had a chance. Of course, we

130

first had to get through Greenidge, Richards & Co., but there was always a prospect of that because their batsmen gave you a chance. Collis King epitomized their batting: a glorious striker of the ball, he played an unbelievable innings in the 1979 World Cup final. He was always looking for runs, and that is good news to a bowler who is happy to trade runs for wickets. They nearly lost the Headingley Test in 1976 because they insisted on hitting the ball all the time – they were 330 for 2 on the first day, only to be all out for just over a hundred more. We battled away to be just sixty-odd behind, and then they collapsed in their second innings, because they all played shots. We needed only 250 to win and, if somebody had been able to stay there and support Tony Greig, we would have won. Their carnival style of batting is great to watch but, for all that, riddled with human frailties.

That series was far closer than it looks on paper. Of course, they had greater talent than we did, but there were occasions when the game really could have gone either way. In the Lord's Test Derek Underwood scared the life out of them, and they trailed us by seventy-odd on the first innings. Then it rained all day Saturday (a cruel irony in such a dry, hot summer), and after that neither side took many risks. In the next Test, they were 26 for 4 on a seamers' wicket, only for Gordon Greenidge to make a magnificent hundred. Even so they only got just over 200, but then England were trapped on a terrible wicket, and their bowlers were just irresistible. At Leeds, we lost by 55 runs when we could easily have won, while at the Oval, Michael Holding's amazing bowling on a flat wicket was the difference. If Underwood had got the opportunity to bowl at them for a little longer at Lord's, he might have established a psychological mastery over them. As it proved, they played him well as the series progressed.

Tony Greig was on a hiding to nothing at the start of the series. He knew he only had pop-guns to answer their heavy artillery, so he opted for a defensive policy to blunt and frustrate them. David Steele, Brian Close, John Edrich and Mike Brearley were simply stopgaps, so that England could hang on until the day when Underwood might snatch a win on a wicket ideally suited to him. It was the same tactic used by Denness, and which had worked against the odds. Our bowling did not look fearsome: Hendrick, Ward, Old, and myself were injury-prone, while Selvey lacked Test class and Snow was not getting any younger. All Greig could do was stick his finger in the dyke and hope for the best. He also indulged in a bit of 'kidology' on the eve of the series which rebounded on him. A great public relations man, Greigy wanted to sell

131

VIV RICHARDS

I first saw Viv Richards in the West Indies in 1974. He batted like a cowboy, trying shots at every ball. To me he looked a typical West Indian flashy batsman; but since then he has become one of the greatest of all time – and he still plays shots at almost every ball.

Batting is a source of pride to Viv. He hates to make a bad shot, or to be tied down and to feel that he is not doing himself justice. He is so cool, so sure of himself, that he can establish a kind of psychological mastery over you. All of us at some stage run in to bowl at him thinking, 'Where the hell's this going to go?' – but many forget that he gives you a chance, more than other great batsmen such as Barry Richards. Viv is so confident that he will try outrageous shots, and he *does* play across the line. His eye is magnificent, of course; but sometimes he will over-reach himself and try something too exotic.

We all have theories about where to bowl at him; and I am now convinced that the only way is to get him champing at the bit through third slip, so I would make do with just one slip, a very deep gully, and a wide third man, and then get the rest trying to stop his shots in front of the wicket. Now I know his footwork and placement of shots are superb, but you have got more chance of worrying him if you double the men available to stop his off-drives and pulls. He might then be tempted to step away and cut the ball through the slips, and then he could play on, or nick a catch to the wicket-keeper. Anything is worth trying when you are up against this kind of talent. Otherwise you just get fatalistic when he hits you for a boundary; and if he for once plays a defensive shot, that gives you a great buzz.

Viv has set standards of professionalism and self-discipline over the years. Despite his genius, he never misses out on the rigorous training that the West Indians indulge in, and he takes great pride in his performance in the field. In my opinion, he has been the greatest all-round fielder of the seventies – he can catch anything close to the bat and his outfielding is astonishing. He ran out three Australians in the World Cup final of 1975. In the last World Cup final, I remember in particular, as a masterpiece of nerve, athleticism, and judgement, his running catch to get rid of Ian Botham. In a John Player League match against Warwickshire, he gave the most brilliant display of fielding I have seen: running round the boundary, hurling in the ball off-balance and getting it right over the stumps, he must have saved thirty runs in forty overs.

The West Indies side is not very impressive when Viv is not around, because his influence on them is nothing but good. He gets very angry at anyone who makes a misfield or throws in badly, and he is strong on proper behaviour. He has absorbed a lot of the better aspects of English cricket from his great friend, Ian Botham. I think Viv may soften the image of the West Indies a little if he becomes captain.

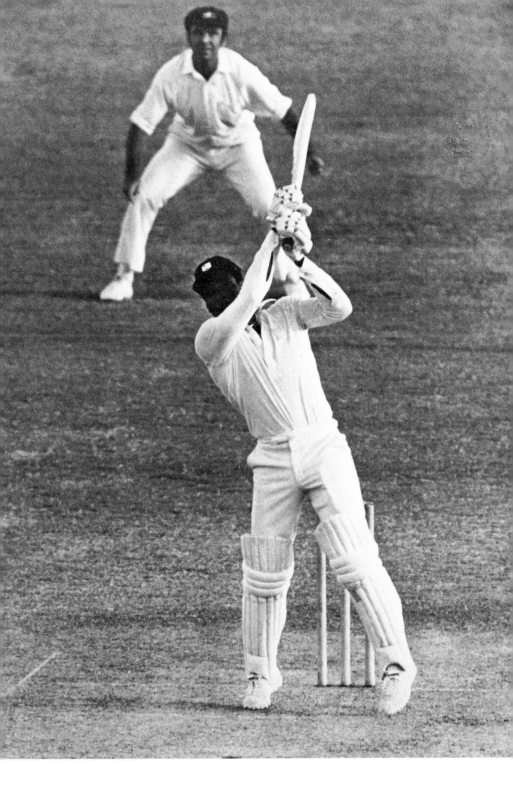

the forthcoming series and, with an eye to the headlines, he told B.B.C. Television that he wanted to make the West Indians 'grovel'. Coming from a white South African, that was an unfortunate turn of phrase, though we all knew what he meant. He wanted to make them struggle and worry about their form by the use of particular tactics. It came out wrong, though, and the racialist implication was like a red rag to a bull, so that Holding & Co. seemed to find extra yards every time Greig came in to bat. Still he took it all in good heart, and I remember a great piece of showmanship from him at the Oval. Greenidge and Fredericks had just hit us all around the park at a rate of six an over, and had then declared. Leading off his side for the last time in the series, Greigy suddenly got down on his hands and knees and crawled for ten yards on his way to the pavilion! The players and supporters loved it, and I think it reflected well on Greigy.

I got back into the England side for the fourth Test at Leeds, starting a run of consecutive Tests that lasted till August 1979. I had been fretting to get back in the early part of that summer, but I was still suffering a series of niggling injuries and things weren't quite right. England were crying out for a fast bowler to fight back against the West Indians, and I remember thinking that I would have loved to have had a crack at them on the Old Trafford wicket. After all, they had been 26 for 4 on the first morning of the match against Mike Hendrick and Mike Selvey, neither of whom were all that quick. If John Snow and myself had been bowling on that wicket, it might have been fun.

I was back for the next Test, even though I'd had little match practice so far. I was even more nervous than normal on that first morning, but it was nice to play in front of a huge, knowledgeable Yorkshire crowd and to get at the batsmen straight away, rather than wait till we had batted. I had troubles with my run-up at the start and, at lunch, they were 140 for no wicket! We pegged them back to manageable proportions, and that first day's play was one of the best I have known in Test cricket. The wicket was ideal for stroke players and for attacking bowlers, the outfield was fast, and wickets fell at a fair rate once the batsmen got overconfident. Greenidge and Fredericks got magnificent hundreds, Richards and Rowe characteristic fifties, and the crowd had their money's worth. In fact that Test was a fantastic game of cricket, with Greig making a tremendous effort to win on the last morning. Alan Ward stayed and added fifty with him without scoring a run, then I came in as last man with 55 needed, only to be out first ball. I was pleased with my bowling: I took eight wickets in the match, including Viv Richards twice, and in the second innings everything clicked for me. It was good to be back.

Even though we lost, we felt some consolation from that Test. They showed their batting rashness in their second innings and, if Collis King had not smashed a quick fifty, they would have lost. Clive Lloyd was not terribly impressive on that last morning when Greig looked as if he might sneak a win – they hardly ever tried to keep him away from the strike. He did not need to look hard for a single to protect Ward, because the West Indies did not seem interested in plugging the gaps. England would always make sure of getting at the tail-ender, but Lloyd seemed happy just to bowl at the established batsman.

The final Test at the Oval soon put our optimism in perspective. For the most part, it was a slaughter in the sun. Viv Richards made 291, they got nearly 700, and we used nine bowlers. I hurt my arm, so I could not bowl very much, and the spinners wheeled away hour after hour. Dennis Amiss made a double hundred that was a triumph of determination and concentration, even though it did not look very good, and finally we were set about 450 to win. Our innings was just a procession against one of the greatest bowling performances I have seen. Michael Holding took fourteen wickets in the match on a featherbed. The ball was hardly bouncing stump high, and the rest of the quick bowlers were ineffectual; but Holding's speed through the air was decisive. He obviously realized that the short-pitched stuff was not going to work, and he pitched the ball up and delivered some devastating yorkers. He clean-bowled nine batsmen, including Tony Greig twice, to his great delight. Greig had a high backlift. Afterwards, he told me how helpless he felt against a bowler of that speed: his stumps were spreadeagled before he knew what was happening.

That performance by Michael Holding is one of the highlights of the seventies for me. It was classic fast bowling with the batsmen beaten by sheer speed. Only Alan Knott and David Steele looked at all comfortable, and poor Chris Balderstone – in his second Test – was twice clean-bowled by Holding for a 'pair'.

So the tour ended with the West Indies recovering a lot of self-confidence after the traumas of Australia. They had become a hard, successful side, and their crowd-pulling potential was enormous. Their Board could never afford to pay them a lot of money, so they seemed ripe for plucking by Kerry Packer. Most of their top players enhanced their reputations in W.S.C., while the lesser ones who were signed up just lined their pockets. When a truce was declared, the West Indies

beat us in the World Cup final and the Benson and Hedges World
Series Cup, and went on to hammer Australia in a three-Test rubber.
The successful formula had been worked out, the players stuck to it,
and to me the umpires and rule-makers did not put many stumbling
blocks in the way of their triumphal progress.

Yet there are still a few nagging doubts in my mind about the West
Indies team. They often did not do themselves justice. They had so
much natural talent, yet they often made hard work of things. They
have struggled on occasions at home: India beat them; New Zealand
managed to draw all five Tests out there; Ian Chappell made light of
the absence of Dennis Lillee to gain a 2–0 victory in 1972–3, while
England's great escape act under Mike Denness flattered us. The
feeling remains that if you can get rid of Viv Richards for nought, they
will fold up. He is so important to them that it all falls apart when he is
not there. Those unsavoury actions in New Zealand probably would
not have happened if Richards had been there, not only because he
would have scored enough runs to make the umpires' mistakes
irrelevant, but also because he would not have allowed his colleagues to

MICHAEL HOLDING

Michael Holding's run-up has been one of cricket's great sights. A beautifully lithe athlete, his smooth acceleration disguises the fact that he is very quick; and only when the ball blurs from his hand do you realize just how very fast he is. In my time, he has been the quickest bowler I have faced, and I do not think I will ever see a better exhibition of intelligent bowling at high speed than at the Oval in 1976.

I have never quite worked out why Holding has not done better at Test level. When you look at the West Indies pace line-up over the years, you must obviously give due praise to Andy Roberts – but Holding always looked as if he was going to be the kingpin. Perhaps he has been too keen to bowl short, to see the batsman hop around a bit. Certainly I thought his performance at the Oval had proved for once and all how ill-advised his short-pitched intimidation was; but since then Holding has not approached that effectiveness. I suppose the demands of World Series Cricket that he should whistle the ball round the batsmen's heads to please the TV viewers had a harmful effect on his bowling technique. Perhaps a season or two in county cricket would have taught him the value of the 'dot' ball – it may look frightening to see the ball bounce yards over the keeper's head, but it does not get anybody out.

---

get carried away. His importance to that side was clear in the way that he had limped around Australia, still making centuries when he should have been resting his injured back. His presence on the field is vital from a playing and psychological point of view.

I think their mediocre performances at home stem from two things: the playing hours and a rivalry amongst the islands. In the West Indies, each Test day only lasts five and a half hours compared with six in England. So a side facing defeat in the West Indies has two and a half hours less to use up in a five-day Test. We might easily have lost two more Tests on the 1974 tour if we had had to face the same amount of playing time as in England. The West Indies have struggled because there has been no corporate unity among their supporters: they have been distracted by petty inter-island jealousies, so that undeserving players occasionally get selected because the match is on their home ground. Otherwise, the spectators would cause trouble. The record books show many examples of players being picked, simply because the Test was in their own back yard. It's a ridiculous situation, but the distance between the islands means that the success of a Barbadian

INTIMIDATION

Brian Close ducks a bouncer from Michael Holding on the Saturday evening at Old Trafford when Test cricket looked a very nasty game indeed. The Manchester wicket in 1976 was a nightmare: the drought had caused corrugated strips to form down the wicket, so that if the ball pitched in a certain area, it just took off. For an hour and a half, Close and John Edrich faced the most sustained barrage of intimidation I have seen. The umpires did not crack down on it, though it was frightening even to watch. No praise can be too high for Edrich and Close – with eighty-four years between them they stood there, occasionally rattled but never buckling. They added 54 in a tremendously brave piece of batting. The futility of the intimidation was borne out on the Monday, when Roberts, Holding, and Daniel pitched the ball up and rolled over all ten English wickets for seventy-odd. Old Trafford 1976 was important not because England lost badly, but because it marked one more step towards giving sustained intimidation the appearance of respectability.

player in a Test is more important to a native of Bridgetown than if a Jamaican wins it for the West Indies. That is why they always do better in England: they are away from the rivalries, they can buckle down to becoming a team, and they do not lack support either.

Their players have contributed greatly to modern Test cricket, but also to its darker moments. More than any other touring side, they seem to need a strong manager, because they do not appear very good at the public relations commitments all Test players now have to meet. They seem unimpressed with turning up for 'Man of the Match' awards, and they seem to think it's all Establishment rubbish. If they continue to play Test cricket in their current ruthless manner, they might be glad of some public relations gestures – because not every fan of Test cricket is fond of 75 balls per hour, bowlers barging into umpires, and teams refusing to take the field after tea because they disapprove of the umpiring. To me, all the majesty of a Viv Richards in full flow cannot disguise the less appealing aspects of West Indies cricket as it enters the eighties.

——8——
PAKISTAN

IN my experience of Test cricket, Pakistan has been the team most afraid of losing. When you consider the talent they have had on offer, that is ridiculous. Many times they have been in winning positions, yet failed to force home the advantage – at Leeds and Edgbaston in 1971 and twice against us on our tour in 1977–8. The same applies to Tests against other countries. It just cannot be a matter of luck: it seems to be accepted by them that a draw is fair enough, but defeat a national disaster. Of all the countries playing regular Test cricket throughout the decade, Pakistan was the only one who did not defeat England – and it is not as if we have been all that fearsome in recent years.

Pakistan has lacked a dynamic captain during my Test career. Intikhab was the best of them: at least he would try to attack on occasions. They have never seemed a particularly happy lot to me: the Pakistan temperament is a somewhat sombre, abstemious and self-disciplined one, and as a result I do not remember many riotous times with the Pakistani players. Their sombre frame of mind sometimes leads to introspection when things are going wrong, and I do not think they are the best side to fight back when the chips are down in a tough Test series. The captaincy seems to have been passed around among most of their top players during the seventies – in itself an admission that the side is not fully together.

The continual wrangles with their Board have not helped their team spirit, either. I recall Sarfraz flying off in a huff during our series out there in 1977–8: he had a long-standing grievance with the Board of Control over expenses, and he said his captain, Wasim Bari, should have taken more notice of his ideas. To me, it was all very silly, and the effect was to rob them of their best bowler for a Test they could easily have won. Another occasion was when the team was disbanded on the eve of the trip to Australia in 1976. They wanted more money, so the Government intervened, sacked the existing selection panel, and eventually gave the players extra cash. Intikhab decided to stay home, while Mushtaq, the captain, and his number two, Asif Iqbal, came out of all

ENGLAND v. PAKISTAN				
Season	Tests	Won by England	Won by Pakistan	Drawn
1971	3	1	0	2
1972–3	3	0	0	3
1974	3	0	0	3
1977–8	3	0	0	3
1978	3	2	0	1

the hassles on top. That was really a forerunner of their involvement with Packer: Mushtaq and Asif were the prime motivators for W.S.C. among the Pakistanis, and I imagine their relationship with their Board of Control had something to do with their defection.

Packer politics sapped the morale of their side just when it looked as if it was going to be a real force in Test cricket. In the space of six months before Packer's plans were announced, Pakistan had won Tests against New Zealand, Australia, and the West Indies. They had their best-ever side – but then they broke up, with half of them going to W.S.C. and the others staying in Test cricket. The Pakistan Board did not like it when their Test side started losing the eminence it had previously achieved, and within a few weeks of the start of W.S.C. there were moves to bring back Asif & Co. The England players on tour in Pakistan took a dim view of that, and we were equally unimpressed with assurances in April 1978 from their Board that other players rumoured to have signed for Packer were untainted by his money. As soon as their short tour of England ended in 1978, Sarfraz, Haroon Rashid, and Javed Miandad admitted that they had signed for Packer. Surprise, surprise – and I felt the same way when the W.S.C. players were flown in to help Pakistan beat India a few months after their England tour had ended. Principles seemed of secondary importance to the Pakistan Board: it was the first team series against India for nearly twenty years, it was perhaps politically important to beat the Indians,

ZAHEER ABBAS

Zaheer Abbas takes his seat in the crowd for the Karachi Test of 1978 after having been flown in by the Packer organization to put pressure on the Pakistan Board to select him for the third Test against England. Zaheer's presence, along with that of Mushtaq and Imran, was embarrassing to the Pakistan players, infuriating to the English, and provocative to the many Pakistani supporters who wanted their best players in the side. That, of course, conveniently overlooked the point that Zaheer and his friends had deliberately opted out of this particular series to play for Kerry Packer.

Zaheer has been a fine batsman, with a monumental reputation in his own country. Over there, he bats as long as he wants on wickets that are slow and low; but in England he has struggled in some seasons. He joined Gloucestershire in 1972, yet he wasn't capped until 1975 – and that is amazing for an overseas player. He took some time to adapt to seaming wickets, and he remains vulnerable to the moving ball. He plays high pace extremely well off the back foot, using the speed of the ball to play his shots in the mode of Glenn Turner. Highly talented, he plays beautifully on the off-side; a very wristy batsman, he is adept at playing down the ball on the rise. I would always back a high-class seamer like Chris Old or Mike Hendrick to trouble him in England, even though he is a big innings man on flat Test wickets.

Apart from Sarfraz and Sadiq, he is the only one of the élite Pakistanis not to have captained his country, an honour that seems to get passed around a lot. I wonder if that troubles him.

---

and therefore Zaheer, Asif, Mushtaq and the rest were needed, even though they had turned their backs on Test cricket the year before. Then, in March 1979, we had a ridiculous situation – the Australians, without their Packer players, played two home Tests against a Pakistan team containing seven, and then eight W.S.C. men. Kerry Packer obligingly released them and, predictably, a grateful Pakistan Board snapped his hand off.

It all seemed so cynical to me. It appeared that Pakistan wanted to avoid heavy and regular Test defeats at all costs. The successive Governments got very involved in Test cricket over there, and past experience has taught me that the presence of politicians in sporting matters tends to cloud the issues somewhat.

Only the West Indies could match the array of fine batsmen turned out by Pakistan, and even then the Pakistanis had the edge in terms of all-rounders, and men like Sarfraz and Wasim Bari were very good

number nine or ten batsmen. Look at this batch: Zaheer, Majid, Mushtaq and his brother Sadiq, Asif, Javed, Haroon, Mohsin Khan, Mudassar, Wasim Raja. They had a really fine wicket-keeper, Wasim Bari, plus three class seamers, Imran, Sarfraz, and Asif Masood. Those three were never quite together at their peak: on the 1971 and 1974 tours to England Imran was still very inexperienced, and it was W.S.C. that sharpened up his pace and control. On the 1978 tour Sarfraz was injury-prone. If they had managed to get all three firing on every cylinder on the same tour, I am sure Pakistan would have won more Tests. In the spin department, they never replaced Intikhab, despite the achievements of Mushtaq and the promise of Iqbal Qasim, Wasim Raja, and Abdul Qadir. The wickets in England just never had enough bounce for their leg-spinners, while Iqbal Qasim lacked control. Intikhab, on the other hand, was the genuine article: a class leg-spinner. He bowled all the variations, had accuracy, patience and the kind of

143

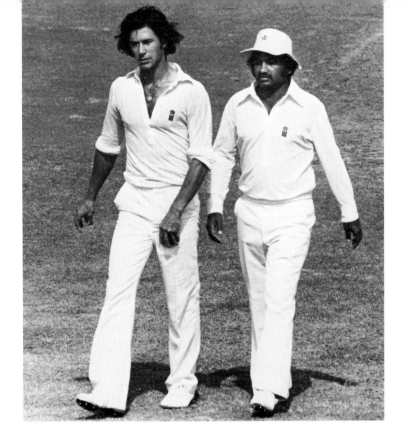

SERVING TWO MASTERS

Imran Khan and Mushtaq Mohammad display the different standards of Pakistan cricket in October 1978. It's Lahore – the second Test against India, just nine months after the Pakistan Board had categorically rejected any moves to select the Packer men for the game against England at Karachi. In a statement bristling with righteous indignation, the Board had talked disparagingly about Kerry Packer, who had 'shown complete disregard to the entire cricket establishment'. The principle that Packer players should remain outside the Test fold was strongly underlined in January 1978. But there followed a disastrous tour of England by their weakened side and, to no one's astonishment, seven Packer players were back in the team for the prestigious series against India. Mushtaq was made captain, and he and Imran showed their feelings for the established order by wearing shirts carrying the World Series Cricket logo, although Mushtaq compromised by sporting a hat topped off by the official Pakistan symbol. The clash of ideals did not matter to either the Board or their players; Pakistan won the Lahore Test by eight wickets, and what could be more important to them than beating India?

philosophical attitude all wrist spinners need. He was also one of the nicest blokes I've met in the game, a man who played cricket the right way; and he can still turn in the goods, after years in cricket. If all the Pakistanis had the same attitude to winning and losing as Inty, they would be a real force to be reckoned with.

Inty was skipper in 1971, when I had my first taste of the powerful Pakistan batting. I was twelfth man, but did a lot of fielding as they batted through till the third morning in the first Test. Mushtaq and Asif got hundreds but the real star was Zaheer. It was an amazing performance to get 274 on his début against England, even though it was a typically docile Edgbaston wicket. His offside play was suberb, and he really lashed into Derek Underwood, smashing him through the on-side. In fact Underwood was dropped in favour of Norman Gifford after that Test, and it was the start of a bad period for him. Only the West Indians and Kim Hughes in Australia have played Underwood as impressively as Zaheer in all my time in the England side.

Rain came to England's rescue in that Test, when Asif Masood was looking as if he would win the game with some class seam bowling in conditions that suited him. The Lord's Test was a wash-out, and in the Headingley Test the Pakistanis were outwitted by Ray Illingworth's shrewd captaincy. It was a low-scoring game, and on the final morning Sadiq and Asif were winning the game. Instead of calmly picking off the runs, they got tied down by Ray's tight field placing and bowling. Asif was stumped giving Gifford the charge, and Sadiq was caught and bowled by Basil D'Oliveira when near his hundred. It was a classic case of the old professional foxing the talented amateurs.

I missed the tour to India and Pakistan in 1972–3, when all three Tests in Pakistan were predictably drawn. Stacks of runs were scored by either side, and there never seemed any elbow-room for a positive result. That has been the pattern all the way through in Pakistan: we have drawn eleven Tests out of twelve over there.

The Pakistanis were now no pushover, compared with the days in the sixties when they seemed to have Hanif Mohammad and ten others. The side Intikhab brought over to England in 1974 was the best, and they were more than a match for us. They batted all the way down to Sarfraz at number ten – one of just four men to reach fifty in the first Test at Leeds, which was left tantalizingly open when rain washed out the last day. In comparison, Chris Old batted at number eight, followed by Arnold, Underwood and Hendrick. At Lord's the Pakistanis were unlucky enough to be caught on a wet wicket ideal for Derek

MAJID KHAN

Majid Khan has been one of the game's most cultured batsmen. A player of almost limitless ability, he seemed to have an eternity to get into position and select one shot from an enviably wide range of options. He never looked in any trouble against the short-pitched stuff, as I found out to my cost at the Oval in 1974, when he made a beautiful 98. It always seemed a surprise when Majid got out.

Judged by his great natural talent, his Test record is disappointing. Presumably this had something to do with casualness, a feeling that it was all rather easy. He certainly made it look so.

A poor captain, both for his country and Glamorgan, he apparently lacked the drive and personality to succeed at the task of threading his way through the jungle of Pakistani intrigues or of welding together the disparate elements of the Welsh team. A deep, serious man, he tried to lead by example, but he never seemed to get the players behind him. He had a bad tactical match in a World Cup match at Edgbaston in 1975 when he failed to beat the West Indies when they had only Murray, Holder, and Roberts left to get over a hundred runs. Sarfraz had finished his allotted spell, and Majid had to bowl his leg-spinners with Wasim Raja and the inexperienced Javed Mian-dad in the closing stages. West Indies won by a single wicket when they should have been well beaten. One of the many examples of Pakistan missing the boat.

Underwood, but lucky too that it rained and ruined our hopes when we had them almost dead and buried. They made a fuss about the rain seeping under the covers, and I did not blame them: if that had happened to us abroad, we would have been equally upset. They allowed themselves to get rattled by the conditions and, if Mushtaq had not held firm for a time against Underwood, they would have lost before the rain saved them. Mushtaq was an exception to the seventies breed of classy Pakistani batsmen – a very shaky starter, but a gutsy fighter, he did not get ruffled. He was used to batting for long periods on flat Pakistani wickets, and he did not throw away his wicket as often as his more flamboyant colleagues. His brother Sadiq has been a good servant as well, although I rate Mushtaq as the better player.

When I was reinstated in the England side in that summer of 1974, I felt as if I had stepped back into a time machine. There was I running in to bowl at Zaheer for hour after hour – shades of Edgbaston in 1971. He got 240 on the flattest Oval wicket imaginable, and he just picked us off at his leisure. Majid had softened us up with a fast 98, hooking and pulling me to his heart's content as I followed instructions to keep on bouncing him. I was quite pleased with my aggressive bowling, but that Oval feather-bed was a nightmare. It suited the temperament of the Pakistanis: they made the game safe with 600, and then tried to bowl us out twice in three days. I was praying that I would not have to bowl again on that wicket, because my feet and toes were still tingling the day after their innings had finished. I really enjoyed the long innings by Dennis Amiss and Keith Fletcher, which sent the Bank Holiday crowd to sleep, but saved the game. There was nothing we could do about that, because if we had given them a reasonable target to chase, their talented batsmen would have strolled home on that pitch.

That Oval Test was a preview of the kind of cricket we had to endure in Pakistan on the 1977–8 tour – except that our batting was not as good as theirs. It was the worst batting England have had in my time and, if the wickets had not been so slow and the Pakistanis so negative, we would have lost the series. Take the first Test at Lahore: Mudassar, normally a stroke-maker, made the slowest century in Test history, and the first two innings of the match were not finished till just after lunch on the final day. Thanks to Mudassar, they batted into the third day to make just over 400! We were left with a rearguard action on our hands, and I added a few for the last wicket with Geoff Miller, who ended up just short of his first hundred in first-class cricket. Eight hundred and

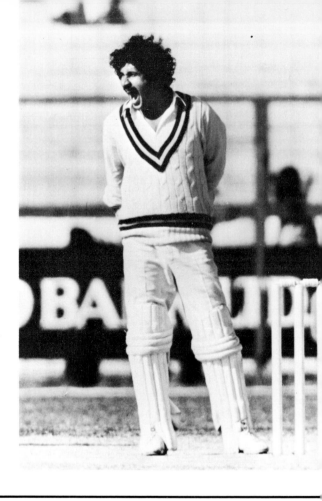

one runs in five days tells its own story. In fact the most stirring event in that Test was the riot started by supporters of Mr Bhutto, who had been imprisoned after a military coup. His wife and daughter turned up to watch the cricket, and predictably that led to a frightening demonstration that lost us an hour's play. The tear-gas came out, the crowds scattered, and it was all very weird. The next day was luckily a rest day, so that the political tensions were eased; but hardly anybody turned up for the rest of the game, and I cannot say I blamed them.

Pakistan could have won the second Test if their captain Wasim Bari had shown any kind of initiative. We had struggled badly against the leg-spin of Abdul Qadir in the first innings. He pitched the ball regularly in the rough caused by my follow-through, and we were so anxious about facing him in the second innings that our manager Kenny Barrington spent a long time in the nets, bowling his leg-breaks at

WASIM BARI

Wasim Bari shows the tedium of playing Test cricket in Pakistan. This picture was taken in the Karachi Test in 1978, when Geoff Boycott's captaincy matched his own in stolidity and lack of initiative, leading to yet another dull draw. The captaincy of his country did not suit a quiet, introspective character like Wasim: the Packer business split the side in two, and he seemed to lack the strength of character to hold things together. And worse, his own splendidly durable wicket-keeping skills declined when he was captain. But as soon as he handed over to Mushtaq, and subsequently Asif, he was back to his best behind the stumps.

For someone so young, Bari has been around a lot: he has made four trips to England for Test series and two more for World Cups. Alan Knott always said he was the best he had ever seen behind the stumps, and certainly he has been a neat, unobtrusive performer, with the ability to dive in front of slip for low catches and to take throws from the outfield with that 'give' of the gloves that stems from sheer class. Only Bob Taylor has had a softer pair of gloves than Bari.

He annoyed me in one way. He has always been a hearty appealer, and he had the habit of throwing the ball up every time he caught it when he stood up to the spinners. This may have been just a habit, but it was unnerving, because it looked as if he was about to appeal. Others would think of joining in and they would lodge an appeal, and the pressure would then be put on the umpire. If the batsman was given out, Bari would say afterwards, 'Well, I didn't appeal', which would overlook the fact that he had sparked things off – and that the umpires in Pakistan are not exactly models of consistency.

Boycott and Brearley. All Wasim Bari had to do was set us a reasonable target in a fair amount of time and, with our frail batting, we would have been struggling. He delayed his declaration ludicrously late, and he left us only a few minutes plus a whole day to get nearly 300 to win. He said the wicket had got slower, but I think he seriously overrated the quality of England's batting. True, Brearley and Boycott batted for the majority of that last day but, with Geoff Miller at number six and Bob Taylor number seven, we might have been in trouble if our opening partnership had been broken early.

Everything about that Hyderabad Test was awful, apart from Haroon Rashid's batting; he got his second hundred in successive Tests against us in the remarkable time, by Pakistan standards, of under three hours. He hit our spinners a long way, and I was impressed by him. I am surprised he has not established himself as a world-class

149

TROUBLE IN KARACHI

Just one of the little things that are sent to try us when we play cricket in Pakistan. It's the third Test at Karachi in 1978 and the crowd, partly in reaction to the boredom of the cricket, decide to induce some excitement into the proceedings with a dust-bag fight. As crowd disturbances go in Pakistan, this was one of the milder ones, and John Lever was sufficiently uninterested in it to carry on bowling. A few minutes previously, this terrace had been crowded. After a time, we got used to things like this – any crowd disturbance after the one at Lahore where tear-gas was used was, in comparison, mundane. If you play often enough in Pakistan, you become immune to the frequent stoppages through crowd trouble, the late starts to the day's play, and the playing on wickets where a positive result is as likely as me getting a Test hundred.

batsman, although his tour of England did show him to be a little loose in defence.

For me there was little excitement in that Test, the crowds were sparse and uninterested and there was nothing to gee us up. The game was fairly tedious, the food left something to be desired, and our hotel was so poor that John Lever was sick as soon as he entered his room because it smelt so much. John was ill throughout his entire stay in Hyderabad, and did remarkably well to keep plugging away in the game.

The final Test at Karachi was another dull stalemate, but there was plenty of action before the game started. Mustaq, Zaheer and Imran appeared at the nets the day before the start, and rumours were rife. In the previous Tests, the crowd had been chanting, 'We want Packer players', and it looked as if the Board and Kerry Packer had the same idea. Those Pakistani players who had played in the first two Tests were strongly against the inclusion of the Packer trio, and the atmosphere between Wasim Bari and Mushtaq was very hostile. As for the England players, we could not work out who was behind the move – was it the Board, or the pro-Packer faction on the Board, was it a piece of 'kidology' by Packer himself, or was the Government behind it all? We had a lot of team meetings, and we were quite clear that we did not want to play against the Packer men. We thought it ridiculous that they should just fly in and take the places of others. We resented the implication that Kerry Packer was running the show and we issued a statement outlining our total objection to the selection of the Packer men. Geoff Boycott had taken over as captain because Mike Brearley had just broken his arm in a one-day game before the Test, and perhaps we would have been less militant if Brearley's calmer influence had been involved. Mike was always more sympathetic to Packer than most of us on that tour – indeed, my views coincided exactly with those of Geoff Boycott. The fact remains that a lot of England players were prepared to put their careers on the line, even though they were on their first England tour. And Mike Brearley agreed that it was not up to Kerry Packer to decide who plays in Test cricket.

Eventually, the Pakistan Board issued a statement which pointed out that the Packer men would not play the next day; they had arrived at Karachi of their own accord, and they had refused to apologize for making themselves unavailable for Tests. The Board went even further by saying that it had ordered the selection committee to concentrate solely on those players who had not sold out to the highest bidder –

151

SARFRAZ NAWAZ

Sarfraz Nawaz is a very fine, underestimated bowler. He bowls a superb line and length, and can do a lot off the seam. Although he has a rather mincing run-up, he gets it right at the end, and his action is very good. For such a big man, he is surprisingly light on his feet, and does not cause much damage to the wicket. His class is measured by the fact that he shares one achievement with Dennis Lillee. Both have bowled out a Test side on a Melbourne wicket where the ball bounces no more than two feet – Lillee in the Centenary Test and Sarfraz in 1979, when he bowled thirty-five overs in the Australian second innings and took nine wickets. The other batsman was run out.

One of the better quickies with the bat, his long reach causes bowlers a lot of trouble. If you bowl anything wide at him, he will get on the front foot and hit you 'on the up' over cover.

A headstrong character, he has done some silly things on the field: there was the beamer he bowled at Tony Greig in the Oval Test of 1974, partly out of frustration at the flat wicket, but also because he did not seem to like Greigy all that much. Then there was the time when he successfully appealed for 'handled the ball' against Australia's Andy Hilditch at Perth in 1979. Sarfraz was still annoyed at Alan Hurst for running out Sikander Bakht when he was backing up at the non-striker's end. So when Hilditch picked up the ball at the non-striker's end and handed it to bowler Sarfraz, he was given out on appeal. That is only the second time it has happened in Test history, and was a legacy from the bad feeling of the previous Test at Melbourne. It was typically hot-headed of Sarfraz, a bloke I always find genial company off the field.

---

quite a contrast to the Board's attitude later that year to the reinstatement of W.S.C. men for the series against India.

We shall never know whether we would have taken the ultimate step if Mustaq and the others had played. Our manager Ken Barrington pointed out that we would be in breach of our contracts, and I suppose we would have been ordered to play by the Cricket Council. The depth of feeling was sincere, and the incident only deepened our disenchantment with Pakistani cricket. That feeling was not diluted by the events in that final Test: there were six L.B.W.s awarded against us in our first innings, and one or two of them were dubious. We batted interminably, and Boycott complained that the bounce was so low that the ball was hitting the bottom three inches of the bat. When the two captains agreed to end the game an hour early, nobody complained.

That Pakistan tour was the most difficult I have been on. There was

little to do, and unlike India, there was nowhere to go. There was no TV, no live music, the food and hotel accommodation were often sub-standard, and all the players saw too much of each other. On the rest day of the Lahore Test, I got hopelessly drunk on whisky with Chris Old just because we were at a loose end – we were well gone by seven in the evening! The crowds were poor, and there was none of the genuine enthusiasm you get in India. The wickets were the slowest and the deadest I have ever played on. I bowled 59 overs in the three Tests, but throughout the lack of bounce was astonishing. You can be the fittest and the best fast bowler in the world, but you will still not get bounce on Pakistan wickets. The political activities were a worry to us too: there was always the feeling that a really nasty riot was due at any stage, and we were well aware that many activists were using the Test arena to display their beliefs. When our plane left the ground at

153

Karachi Airport, bound for New Zealand, I was not sorry to be moving on.

A few months later, we were playing each other again – this time in England, where the wickets gave the bowlers a chance. They were unlucky that it was a terribly wet summer, and they did not do themselves justice. The rumours about Haroon, Javed and Sarfraz signing for Packer affected team spirit, and it all got on top of their captain Wasim Bari. They had some talented young players, such as Haroon, Mohsin Khan, Javed, and Mudassar, who were now out from behind the shadow of Majid and the others who had gone to W.S.C., but the England seam bowlers exposed some technical deficiencies. Hendrick, Botham and I made a good strike force in that summer and this, allied to our superb fielding, meant that the Pakistanis were struggling. Sarfraz bowled only six overs in the first Test because of injury. When he returned to the Leeds Test, it was clear how much they had missed him.

I incurred my share of notoriety in the Edgbaston Test by hitting their night-watchman, Iqbal Qasim, with a bouncer. Predictably I got a lot of stick for what seemed like a very unsporting action, but my critics ignored the fact that Qasim had been holding us up fairly easily for about forty minutes before I let him have it. It seemed wrong to me that a bloke can play you without too much discomfort, secure in the knowledge that you will not bowl him a short-pitched delivery. I was not warned for short-pitched bowling, after all; before I hit Iqbal, I had only been giving him a few shortish deliveries to ruffle him. I thought the outraged reaction was unfair, and it led to the farce of both sides nominating non-recognized batsmen whom the bowlers would not bounce. I was one of them, but I should not have complained if I had got the treatment – I would have worn a helmet or tried to get out of the way. I agree that umpires should clamp down on systematic and persistent intimidation, but I do not think I was guilty of that at Edgbaston. I did make one mistake, though: when I hit Qasim, I stayed away from him, because I felt that if I had seen his blood, then my concentration would have been impaired and my bowling would have suffered. That was wrong – I should have looked concerned, gone down the wicket to him, and made it clear I was sorry he had been hit. It was bad public relations on my part, and I imagine that is why I was criticized so much, rather than because I'd bowled a nasty ball at an obdurate tail-ender.

Ian Botham dominated this series. He made two powerful hundreds,

A DAMP OUTLOOK

The moment when it dawned on the Pakistan team in 1974 that they were going to have to face Derek Underwood on a rain-affected wicket. It is the Monday morning of the Lord's Test and rain has seeped through the covers to reveal a damp patch on a perfect length for Underwood. Mushtaq photographs the evidence while (from left to right) England captain Mike Denness, umpire David Constant, Pakistan's Asif Iqbal, and their captain, Intikhab, survey the scene. The Pakistanis accused the ground authorities of 'appalling negligence and incompetence in not covering the wicket adequately'; and with Underwood taking 6 for 9 later that day, one can understand their anger. When rain prevented any play on the final day, many felt justice was done.

and at Lord's produced a remarkable piece of swing bowling in their second innings. He went on at the Nursery End only so that I could change ends, but he swung the ball to an astonishing degree. Of course, he is a natural swing bowler, and on this day everything was in smooth working order, and he demoralized the Pakistanis – all this on a cloudless day, with a ball that had been changed after the original one had gone out of shape.

Many critics slated Pakistan after this series, but I think their memories were rather short. They had many talented players in their side, but nothing went right. They had a very long tail, their batsmen lacked experience of English conditions, and the weather gave them no chance of getting vital match practice before the Tests started. In contrast, England had a stronger side than just a few months earlier in Pakistan – Botham had been ill over there and had not played in a Test, while David Gower and Graham Gooch had strengthened the batting and improved the fielding still further. Bob Taylor was superior to Wasim Bari behind the stumps, while we had several all-rounders and, with Phil Edmonds batting nine or ten, a short tail. We were forging ahead confidently, and went on to beat New Zealand 3–0 and Australia 5–1 inside nine months. So perhaps we were strong, while Pakistan were unlucky.

Pakistan have been the 'nearly' men of Test cricket. They have had more class players than most and if only they could shake off this passive attitude to cricket, they would be a better unit. Perhaps the ravages of Kerry Packer upset them more than most countries, but if so I have no sympathy for them, because I believe they lacked integrity at times. I do not pretend to understand why players from a different class cannot get on with others in the side, nor why someone from the north of the country does not warm to a player from the south. Nor do I understand why their Governments have often seen fit to interfere in the running of the Test team. Pakistan have seemed a divided team to me, and perhaps those divisions have sapped their will to win. In the World Cup both in 1975 and in 1979, they did not seem to know how to win crucial games – at Edgbaston in 1975 when the West Indies scraped home by one wicket after needing over a hundred to win with just two wickets left; and then at Leeds in 1979 when we beat them by fourteen runs. We were right in the cart with eight down for just over a hundred, but they let Bob Taylor and myself off the hook and we added forty-odd. Even then, 166 was surely a doddle for a side containing men like Majid, Zaheer and Javed, with Imran Khan coming in at number nine. True, Mike Hendrick bowled superbly, but they batted badly, and Mike Brearley outwitted Asif in the tactical stakes. Then in the semi-final, Pakistan put up a great performance against the powerful West Indian bowlers. Majid and Zaheer put them in contention with a brilliant partnership, but when Zaheer was out, they just subsided gently.

Perhaps if Pakistan had won the World Cup in 1979, it might have ushered in a feeling of self-belief and positive leadership for them. They certainly do not lack the talent.

9

INDIA

I wish every side played Test cricket in the same way as India. I have always found them extremely charming and sporting men, for whom sportmanship is still not a word to be sneered at. The crowds out there are very enthusiastic and, unlike those in Australia, they do not just turn up when they are on top. And they give full credit to the opposition as well.

They are my favourite Test side to play against, and that is not just because their players are generally super blokes. I happen to believe that spin bowling means good, interesting cricket. When the ball is slightly on top, there is change and challenge in the game, and the best batsmen can still come through. Skill with bat and ball becomes of prime importance. In the last two or three years India has unearthed a fine seam bowler in Kapil Dev, and it may well be that his example and the fact that Indian wickets are getting faster will encourage more youngsters to try seam bowling, rather than wheeling away for hour after hour. Before Kapil Dev came onto the scene, the Indian opening bowlers simply turned their arms over: men like Solkar, Abid Ali, and Gavaskar were used to get the shine off the ball, and then the spinners would come on to tease, frustrate and delight many.

Only one Test series in England during the past decade has been dominated and won by spin bowling: the 1971 series, when India snatched their first win in England at the Oval. It is true that the weather favoured India during that wet summer, but many neutrals rightly enthused over the artistry of the Indian spinners. Bedi, Chandrasekhar, Venkat and Prasanna were all of widely differing styles, and they took around 750 Test wickets amongst them. India could perm any three from this quartet, and it was not until the Madras Test against the West Indies in 1979 that only one of them played – Venkat. By 1980, Bedi was in decline and Chandra and Prasanna had retired, but they left behind some happy memories for spectators and players.

Chandra bowled fast leg-breaks, and his withered right arm, stem-

ENGLAND v. INDIA				
Season	Tests	Won by England	Won by India	Drawn
1971	3	0	1	2
1972–3	5	1	2	2
1974	3	3	0	0
1976–7	5	3	1	1
1979	4	1	0	3

ming from polio, didn't seem to affect his ability. Bedi was a beautiful artist: a left-arm spinner with all the traditional virtues of flight, variety and turn. Venkat was an off-spinner in the English mould; Alan Knott rated him very highly, and certainly his length and line were invariably accurate. I preferred Prasanna's off-breaks: he had a low arm, but he imparted a huge amount of spin. He had the leg-spinner's attitude to someone getting after him. He would smile, lick his fingers, and keep tempting him. None of this stuff about keeping it tight and frustrating the attacking batsmen; he would accept the challenge. That is why he could bowl out sides on good batting wickets, whereas Venkat would need assistance from the pitch before he could really make the ball talk.

The Indian philosophy towards life in general equipped these four bowlers for their craft. They do not believe in rushing around in India, and this inherent patience is a vital ingredient in a successful spinner's make-up. This has also been a feature of the Indian batting when they have faced huge totals in the last innings of a Test on a good batting wicket. Their fine effort at the Oval in 1979, when they almost won after being set a target of over 400, was typical, based on calmness and technical skill.

The balance of the sides has never quite been right with India, because they have specialist players. Only Venkat of their spin quartet has been a presentable batsman, so that the tail started early in their side. Kapil Dev's all-round ability has helped in that respect, but they

159

SUNIL GAVASKAR

Sunil Gavaskar during his astonishing innings of 221 at the Oval in 1979. It was an amazing feat of concentration and certainty of stroke play, and it really should have won India the match. It confirmed Gavaskar as one of the great batsmen, which is exactly what he promised to be when he made four hundreds against the West Indies in 1970–1.

He first came to England with a glittering reputation after those huge scores, but he was intelligent enough to realize that you do not become a top-class batsman until you have mastered English pitches. He was a blocker in 1971, and only a little less sedate in 1974; then he finally showed his true quality in 1979. Like Glenn Turner and Geoff Boycott, he worked out his defensive technique before broadening his range of strokes. How sensible – I just wish our younger English batsmen would take note.

Extremely pleasant, he nevertheless seems a stronger character than his brother-in-law, Viswanath. He will speak his mind to the selectors, and he has had his disputes with them. Perhaps that is why he has not captained India as often as he should. I remember an amazing innings he played at Bangalore in 1977 when he had had a

difference of opinion with the selectors: he went straight out and slogged against us, and was soon out.

He has a strong sense of destiny, and maintains he knew that he would become Ian Botham's hundredth Test wicket at Lord's in 1979. Perhaps that explains why he batted so rashly in that famous over, because he might have been out three times before Mike Brearley caught him. He says he had a premonition, and nothing would alter his view that he was the chosen batsman.

Only once has he annoyed me: at Bombay, when he opened the bowling and blatantly followed through to scar the wicket for the spinners. We had enough to contend with without a deliberate tactic like that, and he was told so in forthright terms. That is the only time I have known him to be other than sporting and likeable.

In India – particularly in Bombay – he is a superstar. If he decided to go into politics, he would be in charge of the country for sure. There is no chance of that: he is going to be around for a while longer – at least until he breaks some more batting records. And the fact that he has got so near Bradman's record of Test hundreds within just a decade only underlines what a terrific player he is.

have always needed wicket-keepers who can bat a bit. Kirmani and Engineer have been more than adequate at both tasks. Engineer was a typical Indian cricketer – happy, smiling, no day was too long for him. He stood up to the spinners very well for a number of years; it must have been difficult to adjust your technique to their differing subtleties. As a batsman, he loved to crack the ball, and he made good Test match runs. He was one of the overseas players who did a lot for their county, both on and off the field, and he was popular in Lancashire. Kirmani took over the gloves. I have always been impressed with him: he never let himself be intimidated, and I particularly remember his superb hooking of me in the 1976–7 tour, when I was bowling really fast.

There was another reason why the Indian spinners prospered: close fielding. The wicket-keeping was good, while Viswanath, Wadekar and Gavaskar have been very good in the slips and they have had two superb short-legs. Solkar was outstanding, while Yajuvendra Singh is the best I have seen in that position. In his first Test against us he took seven catches, and some of them were astonishing. Where India have fallen down is in their fielding away from the bat: Bedi and Prasanna, for example, were nothing if not stately on the run, and only Kapil Dev has looked really impressive in the outfield. I shall never forget a

161

GUNDAPPA VISWANATH

Gundappa Viswanath is a delightfully well-balanced batsman with a great record at Test level. Not quite as good a player as his brother-in-law, he is more of a cutter and deflector, whereas Gavaskar plays more strokes off the front foot. Nimble on his feet, he is one of those players whom you must try to get out early. His defence is excellent, his temperament serene, and he gives the bowler little encouragement. Having been brought up on placid Indian wickets, he has learned about the game at a relaxed pace, and he knows exactly what he can achieve during an innings.

Since the Georgetown Test on the 1970–1 tour of the West Indies, he has played in every Test involving India right through the decade – a tremendous record of fitness and consistency. A modest, charming character, he has a deserved reputation for both his cricketing ability and his sportsmanship – just ask Bob Taylor.

wonderful stop and pick-up by him in the Jubilee Test at Bombay; after he had thrown down the stumps off-balance, I turned to Mike Brearley and said: 'I can just see a camel like me managing that!'

I enjoyed watching the 1971 Indians so much that I was really looking forward to going out there on the 1972–3 tour. But I was not selected, and that remains one of the biggest disappointments of my career. I was twelfth man for the Oval Test against Australia, and Ray Illingworth had told me I would be going. 'India's a young man's tour,' he said, and confirmed that he was not available. So Tony Lewis took over, and I sat in my flat at Birmingham and heard the team being read out on the radio. I can still remember my sadness as the list got to Barry Wood's name in alphabetical order and I had been passed over. All the lads who went on that tour said it was good value, even though we lost 2–1. I had been hooked on spin bowling since that tremendous last Test at Sydney in 1971 when Ray Illingworth and Derek Underwood had bowled us to victory, and I was looking forward to seeing those great Indian spinners in action on their own wickets. Between them, Bedi and Chandra took 60 wickets; but I had to wait another four years before I got to India.

Before then, they had a most unhappy tour of England. The weather in 1974 was no better than in their triumphant year of 1971, but they could never get started. The fielding declined, Chandra was injured, and Bedi was overbowled, averaging nearly sixty overs in all three Tests! The England batsmen picked up cheap runs, while the Indians seemed to go into their shell, accepting that the Fates were against them. A more positive captain might have helped, but Wadekar seemed distracted by his own poor batting form.

Two years later, the captaincy had gone to Bedi when we travelled to India for one of the most enjoyable Test series I have known. That opinion has nothing to do with the fact that we won 3–1. We were a happy side. I bowled consistently fast and, unusually for a quick bowler in India, took a lot of wickets. Our captain Tony Greig and the manager Ken Barrington worked on my approach to the wicket by getting me to straighten it out a little and, apart from a slow start to the tour (caused by the inevitable stomach troubles), I felt fit and confident.

I was enormously impressed by the crowds in India. They were so appreciative and individually polite whenever we were approached. The support was remarkable, with huge crowds at every Test ground. In the second Test at Calcutta, a crowd of 60,000 turned up on the last

BHAGWAT CHANDRASEKHAR

Bhagwat Chandrasekhar won India's first series in England when he bowled out Ray Illingworth's side at the Oval in 1971 with a brilliantly controlled display of leg-spin. For the rest of the decade he baffled a succession of Test batsmen with his speed off the pitch: they would be shaping up to pull an imagined long-hop, only to find it fizz through and trap them L.B.W. I was always amazed at the speed he could impart to the ball with that withered right arm of his, and his economical Test returns gave the lie to the theory that leg-break bowlers are expensive. No great bowler is expensive, because he will always get a stack of wickets throughout the world.

He bowled beautifully in 1977–8 in Australia, when he and Bedi did their bit for traditional cricket in the face of the brash World Series Cricket version. It must have been satisfying for the purist to watch Bedi and Chandra spinning away for hours, using their brains, craft, and experience; while on Channel 9, fine batsmen were ducking the thunderbolts. I know which brand of cricket I would have watched.

I played in Chandra's last Test at Edgbaston in 1979. He had achilles trouble, but he had to play because Bedi had dropped out with a stiff neck. It was sad to see Chandra struggling, and he went for over a hundred on a flat track without taking a wicket; those who missed him in his prime were unlucky. A happy, delightful man, he was the worst Test batsman I have seen – but a wonderful bowler, and the kind of guy who has become a rarity in Test cricket.

day, even though India was in a hopeless position, needing another handful of runs to avoid the follow-on, with just a couple of wickets in hand. When they managed it, the roar was like the Cup Final at Wembley! Yet they gave us a marvellously warm reception when Tony Greig led us on our lap of honour round the ground. Greig's sense of public relations was immaculate on that tour: right from the start, he handled the Press conferences in the right way, praising the Indian players and their umpires, even though we knew that the umpires have usually not been the greatest. He would lead us out before the start of play, and we would wave to the huge crowd and get them warming towards us. Greigy gave full rein to Derek Randall's sense of fun. He allowed Randall to perform cartwheels on the field, go through his Charlie Chaplin routine, and try anything to brighten up the day. In a land where starvation, deprivation, and misery are common to millions, it was the right thing to do. We enjoyed giving pleasure to so many, and it was terrific to experience the appreciation of the Indian public.

Bishen Bedi could not be anything but genial as captain of the opposition, although he did get a little disgruntled and tetchy after we went 3–0 up in the series. I got the impression that some of them were fed up of being the whipping-boy halfway through the series, and they certainly increased the number of optimistic appeals – but generally, it was an enjoyable series to play in. They were mostly charming in defeat: Chandra would come into our dressing-room, all smiles, have a drink, and in his halting English he would do his best to congratulate us, while men like Kirmani and Viswanath were great as well.

We started off the series with an innings victory to give us our first Test win since New Zealand in 1976. John Lever, on his début, was the architect, getting a half-century in a long partnership with Dennis Amiss and then bowling beautifully. We used an Indian-manufactured ball which swung quite alarmingly. John's county captain, Keith Fletcher, told him to aim at him at first slip as he bowled over the wicket; and sure enough, the ball did all sorts of things, and he picked up three L.B.W.s in the first innings when it swung in very late. One feature of that Test was a fascinating duel between Derek Underwood and Sunil Gavaskar: Underwood bowled nearly fifty overs, and Gavaskar's class, patience and defensive skills had me full of admiration. I only bowled nine overs in that innings, but I could not have cared less – and when I got up the next day to go and see the Taj Mahal I carried around a pretty sore head.

BISHEN BEDI

Bishen Bedi adorned cricket with the beauty of his bowling, his exotically colourful headgear, and his generous nature. I knew him to be ruffled only once: during the 1976–7 tour by England, where a series of defeats overcame that philosophical nature and caused him to make some rash claims which I am sure he later regretted.

As a man and a cricketer, he could not have been more unlike the modern breed of West Indian players, and he was incensed at their intimidation at Kingston in 1976. Five Indians were absent hurt and Bedi more or less gave them the match in protest against the short-pitched hostility that had led to the injuries. Test cricket in its ruthless garb did not seem to suit Bedi: he preferred the action to be more sedate, with brainpower and skill outweighing muscle and games-manship.

I could never applaud a batsman when he has hit me for six in the way that Bedi has done many times; I would storm back to my mark, feeling humiliated and angry. But when it was my turn to hit *him* for six, he would stand there smiling and clapping – and it was genuine, because he liked a batsman to take him on; he hated blockers. He would rather take 5 for 80 in 30 overs than 3 for 50 in the same number of overs. Despite his success in county cricket, the tougher, limited-overs version of the three-day game in England did not really suit him, and it was no surprise when Northants and he parted company. A poor fieldsman and batsman, he was a specialist cricketer of great gifts; yet modern cricket does not seem to want people like him.

Eventually India turned him into both a strike bowler and a stock bowler and he was worn down. I count myself lucky to have played against him.

I had more work to do in the second Test at Calcutta, where I bowled very quickly on a wicket that turned straight away. Tony Greig played a remarkable innings, batting for hour after hour in the knowledge that the ball would turn even more later on. Time was on our side because we had bowled them out quickly in their first knock, so Greigy just stayed there. He had a fever, and after every session he would have to lie down and then change his clothes. Early in his innings he mistimed a drive off Chandra and became convinced that the pitch was not a stroke-making one, so he got all his runs off the back foot. It was laborious, but there was not a peep of disapproval out of the huge crowd. They realized that it was engrossing cricket, that the ball does not always have to be knocked out of the ground at regular intervals – and their reception for Greigy was fantastic.

So we were 2–0 up already and, by this time, Bishen Bedi was getting a little down. The defensive play of our batsmen was frustrating him, too – on the last tour, many of our blokes had tried to hit their way out of trouble, only to get out. This time we occupied the crease for long periods, and just blocked and blocked. Bishen hated that; he loved the batsmen to attack him, because that improved his chances of tempting them and luring them to destruction. Perhaps that frustration explains why he made the allegations in the third Test that led to what was known as 'the Vaseline Incident'.

It was all very innocuous, and the whole thing was blown completely out of proportion. It started innocently enough: John Lever and myself were suffering in the humidity of Madras. Both of us had fairly long hair, and the sweat was getting into our eyes. Our physiotherapist Bernard Thomas had the idea of putting strips of gauze over our eyebrows, stuck on with Vaseline, to direct the sweat away from our eyes. They failed to work, and after five minutes I discarded mine. When John ran up and bowled, the gauze strip slipped down and he threw it away. The umpire picked it up as he walked back, and noticed that it was covered in grease. That got to Bedi, and the next day the 'Lever's a cheat' banners were out in force. The ball was taken away and analysed, and Lord's got involved; but Ken Barrington smoothed things over, and the heat was taken out of the situation. The whole thing was completely innocent, even though Vaseline inevitably got onto the ball, and that would make it swing.

I think the fact that we won the toss was more crucial in our victory in that Test, rather than any amount of Vaseline. After Brearley and Greig had helped give us a reasonable total, we shot them out on one of the quickest wickets I have ever bowled on – an astonishing contrast to previous ones in India. It was rock-hard, with patches of grass on it, and the Indian batsmen were not exactly resolute. By a strange chance I was hit under the chin while batting against Chandra, and I had to have four stitches. Then I broke Vengsarkar's hand when a ball lifted up nastily. Before we knew it, we had won the series, and the Indians looked demoralized.

They pulled one back in Bangalore, where again the toss was decisive. Chandra, Bedi and Prasanna were sitting pretty, and they did not let go this time. Three remarkable innings were played in that Test: two of superb technique by Gavaskar and Viswanath, and another which was the most amazing I have ever seen. Alan Knott went in with England in a hopeless position in the final innings of the match. The ball was turning almost two feet, yet Knotty made an astonishing 81 not out. He would use his nimble footwork to get down the wicket and hit the spinners over the top; then he would wait for the quicker ball, lean back and cut it. I batted with him for a time at the end, and I marvelled at his brilliance. If someone could have stayed with Knotty, he might even have won that game off his own bat.

Another Englishman played a superb innings in the last Test – this time a defensive one. Keith Fletcher saved the game for us that final day. We needed just over 200 in four hours, and either side could have won an absorbing game. Fletcher guided us through, and we had three wickets in hand and an honourable draw at the close. I sat in our dressing-room that afternoon, not daring to watch a ball in case I brought us bad luck. I had taken a look at just one ball, and Roger Tolchard was out! We held on, and in the process proved that an exciting, fascinating cricket match can also be a draw. Prasanna and Bedi bowled more than 150 overs between them in the match, and Underwood over 70. I did not take one wicket, but my version of what constitutes a good cricket match does not depend on how well I have done in it. I fielded near to the bat for most of the game and thoroughly enjoyed the skills of Gavaskar – always getting the right angles of the bat to the ball to avoid popping one up – and the exhilarating footwork and stroke play of Patel. It really was tremendously engrossing, and proved the point that it is a far better game when the spinners prosper: the fielders have to concentrate more because they know the spinner is bowling to his field with plans in his mind, while the batsmen need to keep their wits sharp and look out for the loose ball on which to capitalize.

It was fascinating to see how calm the Indian spinners were, apart from Bedi when our blocking tactics occasionally got to him. They did not get flustered and try to bowl too quickly; they would stroll back to the mark and keep chipping away, content to match their skills against our batting. They had been playing for a very long time, and they knew their capabilities. One of the best things about this series was the fact that the bat did not dominate, as it sometimes does in India. No side made over 500 in an innings, and with the ball slightly on top and the wickets occasionally tricky, it meant that batting had to be skilful to survive and prosper – and that is what cricket should be all about. I just hope we would have been as charming in defeat as most of the Indians.

It was a happy tour for us, and I am sure that it was not just the fact that we won that caused that. We all took back many happy memories from India. Mike Brearley, in particular, fell in love with the place; the tempo of life out there suited his personality, he liked the fact that you could stand and talk to someone without being hustled along. The hotels were magnificent, a mixture of the old and the new, and the food superb. Delhi is a city of tremendous history; Madras has its own seaside charm despite the humidity; while Bangalore has the most beautiful climate, warm without being too oppressive. All the grounds had their own distinct atmosphere, and we responded to the enthusiasm of those huge crowds.

Many critics said that was the weakest Indian side in its Test history, which was surely stretching things too far and not giving England due credit. Their fielding could not compare with ours, with Randall, Lever, Barlow, and Greig consistently superb; and although it is true that their great spinners did not win many games, they were nevertheless very dangerous. We were lucky that Greig, Underwood, Knott, Amiss, and Fletcher had learned much from the previous tour four years earlier. They had worked out a passive way of playing the spinners which was comparatively successful. The biggest problems the Indian spinners faced were lack of support in the field, and not enough runs to bowl at. Only Viswanath and Gavaskar looked true Test class as batsmen. To me India looked far worse under Wadekar in 1974 in England; in their own country, they could always expect to have a good chance.

The saddest thing about the Indian tour to England in 1979 was the decline of their spinners. Chandra, Venkat, and Bedi took thirteen wickets amongst them in four Tests, and the admirable performances of Kapil Dev made me think we were at the end of an era, and that seam bowling was beginning to dominate even Indian cricket. Kapil Dev and his opening partner, Ghavri, bowled many more overs than the three spinners and, although they were easily the best opening bowlers India have possessed, the fact that they were overbowled suggests that a new mood of realism is sweeping through Indian cricket. Certainly the way that wickets have got slower and slower throughout the world has not helped the Indian spinners that much, and it is all credit to their skills that they have been such an adornment for so long.

The weather saved India from a series of heavy defeats in 1979, but it did not prevent them from showing their resilience when they were really up against it. It happened at Lord's, where they faced a deficit of over 300 and calmly batted out the last day, with Vengsarkar and Viswanath making excellent hundreds; and we saw the same durability at the Oval, where they made a tremendous effort at the target of 438. They finished nine runs short with two wickets in hand, and really should have won. We had lost Mike Hendrick with an injured shoulder; the wicket got flatter and flatter, and I was out to pasture down at third man, hardly able to put one foot in front of the other after bowling a lot of overs. If India had been more experienced in one-day cricket, they would have coasted home; with so many wickets in hand, they were dictating things, and all they needed to do was pick off ones and twos. Gavaskar got out at a crucial stage after one of the great innings of the decade, and they panicked and started slogging. It was wrong to send in Kapil Dev early to smash a few, while a superb player like Viswanath dropped down the order. Ian Botham kept us in that game near the end with three wickets, a catch, and a run-out, but the real giant was Gavaskar. Apart from playing and missing about three times just after he reached his hundred, his double century was flawless. In the end, fatigue got him out.

By the time we met up again with the Indians in the Jubilee Test at Bombay, they were shattered. They had played seventeen Tests in seven months and seemed out on their feet. The crowd was surprisingly poor but, considering that it was the third Test to be staged there in three months, there probably was not all that much money left to go around. The Jubilee Test was a very grand, old-fashioned affair, with the usual crop of former captains being wheeled out and an air of respect for the traditions of Test cricket. A gesture from the new Indian captain, Viswanath, was in keeping with those traditions: he recalled Bob Taylor after he had been given out, caught behind. The umpire stuck his finger up very quickly, and 'Vishy' did not agree. It was a fine gesture of sportsmanship, which probably cost India the match, because Taylor and Botham then forged an important partnership. There was another bizarre umpiring decision later in the match when Boycott was adjudged caught behind off Kapil Dev. Only the leg-side fielders appealed, but the finger went up; Boycott affected not to have noticed, so the umpire put his finger down, Boycott stayed put and went on to yet another not-out! John Lever had some uncomplimentary things to say about the umpiring in this match – he reckoned he had had four plumb L.B.W.s turned down.

Although we won handsomely by ten wickets, the main difference between the two sides was provided by Ian Botham and Bob Taylor. They dominated the match: Botham with a century and thirteen wickets, Taylor with a dogged supporting innings and the world record

171

total of dismissals in a Test. Without these two, it could have been anybody's game. The sardonic reaction of Derek Underwood to meeting up with a seamer's wicket in India of all places can well be imagined!

I took no part in the Jubilee Test, being stricken low with a virus. I could only make it to the ground for an hour before I tottered back to the hotel and watched the game on TV. It was good to watch the cricket uninterrupted and not to have to sit through seventeen minutes of adverts every hour, as in Australia. The commentary team were genuinely enthusiastic too, and even with half of what they said being in Hindi, I found the coverage infinitely preferable to the inanities of Channel 9's commentators in Australia.

I got the impression that Test cricket still meant a lot to people in India, although they clearly had got involved in far too many series recently. Interest is still very strong indeed in India: an amazing crowd

VISWANATH AT THE JUBILEE TEST

The moment that lost the 1980 Jubilee Test for India, yet confirmed their reputation for sportsmanship. Bob Taylor had scored just seven when he was given out caught behind by Kirmani off Kapil Dev. Taylor dragged himself away from the crease in astonishment that the umpire's finger had shot up so rapidly; but India's captain, Viswanath, then intervened. He asked the umpire to accept that the appeal had been withdrawn. Taylor was allowed to stay, and England – at that time 85 for 5 – advanced to a lead of 50 on the first innings. The stand between Taylor and Ian Botham added 171, and turned the game. Botham and Taylor finally won the game with their performances in India's second innnings, but this big stand was the turning point of the match.

Bob Taylor was probably wrong to make such a show of disapproval when he was given out, although I suppose it was a natural reaction. The action of Viswanath was wholly admirable, although it will perhaps establish a precedent for other batsmen to hang around after being given out controversially, in the hope that the fielding captain will intervene. Then we might get a game of bluff and double-bluff. Basically, if we do not accept the umpires' decisions, the game will fall apart.

Viswanath's action recalled that of Rod Marsh in the Centenary Test three years earlier, when he recalled Derek Randall. That gesture by Marsh came as a bit of a shock, and it is indicative of the respect England's players have for Viswanath that his intervention seemed wholly typical.

of 55,000 turned up to see Ian Botham and Graham Gooch win a double-wicket competition three days before the Jubilee game. We were still treated like film stars by the locals, and it was a pleasant change from the harshness of Australia.

Although India had a rocky passage in the mid-seventies, they ended the decade with a compact side. Dilip Doshi, my Warwickshire team-mate, had replaced Bedi as the left-arm spinner; and, although it is wrong to make comparisons, Dilip soon showed he was a wicket-taker. Kapil Dev had become a Test all-rounder, completing the double in an impressively short time. With Kirmani batting number eight and Ghavri at nine, there was more depth to their batting. They had two of the best batsmen in the world: Gavaskar and Viswanath. Vengsarkar, too, was a high-class one. The fielding had improved, with Roger Binny and Kapil Dev brilliant in the deep. So it would be wrong to place too much emphasis on India's defeat in the Jubilee Test; after all, they had

INDIAN CROWDS

Bob Woolmer experiences the adulation of a cricket-mad country in
1977. The Indian public would wait for hours outside our hotels just
to get a look at us on that tour. They were patient and unfailingly
polite, and treated us like film stars. People would come hundreds of
miles with their families just on the off-chance of getting an introduc-
tion to one of the players. If one of us would pose for a photograph for
the family album, their joy was complete. It was easy to warm to the
sincere enthusiasm of these people, especially after the boorishness of
many cricket followers in other parts of the world. The Indian cricket
supporter is fair-minded, devoted to the game, and amazingly tolerant of long, boring periods when nothing seems to be happening.
Their crowds mirror the image of the home side – and in India, both
the crowds and the cricketers are delightful.

174

just beaten Australia 2–0 (without the Packer players, admittedly), and Pakistan by the same margin. Six Packer players had been in the defeated Pakistan side, and that must have been sweet for India.

If only India could sort out the captaincy issue, they could go from strength to strength. I feel that Gavaskar is the strongest and the most decisive at the job, but he has his ups and downs with the Board of Control. Wadekar and Venkat have been too introspective as captains, while Bedi seemed preoccupied with his bowling. Viswanath is a rather retiring individual also, and perhaps his more dynamic brother-in-law is the right man. Certainly Gavaskar need never worry about whether he is in the side just for his captaincy!

It remains to be seen whether India eventually gets dipped in the dye of commercialization after their trip to Australia, which will involve all the overkill and stage-management for the benefit of TV that we have endured over there. I hope that India does not lower its standards. I was encouraged by the universal praise for Viswanath's act of sportsmanship in the Jubilee Test. In other countries, a captain who did that would be given a hard time if he lost the Test. What worries me is that a generation of cricket-lovers might soon be growing up without having had the sheer pleasure of seeing those marvellous Indian spinners. It would be nice to think that the decline of Bedi & Co. will not break the chain of tradition that breeds slow bowlers.

────10────

CRICKET IN
THE 1980s

AS I enter my third decade in first-class cricket, I am convinced of one thing – the game is not as enjoyable as it was when I first started. I am a lot richer, in common with a few other England players who just happened to be around at the right time. Although the game is a lot more commercial, I do not think it is more professional, nor do we work as hard as we should do for our money. Of course, the travelling is very hard going; and, although the word 'pressure' is over-used nowadays, nevertheless I still suffer badly from nerves before and during a big match. The modern player is well rewarded for the privilege of playing the game he loves: and perhaps we have had it all rather easy recently.

In my view, there is a soft under-belly on the body of English cricket, and that is one of the reasons why we are still a mediocre Test side. Not enough of our talented batsmen are prepared to emulate the example of Geoff Boycott and work out exactly how to bat on all wickets. The money is so good that there is a subconscious feeling that there is always going to be a Santa Claus around to bail us out with the readies – but those of us lucky enough to have kept going could spend a long time ticking off a list of the talented players who did not make it because they thought it all too easy after a couple of good seasons.

Attitude apart, the rules need altering drastically if England are to prosper again in Test cricket. In the county championship, sides are overloaded with overseas players who get the new ball or the best batting places because of their prowess. Under the hundred-over limitation, which existed until the 1981 season, number five or six batsmen usually got a fifteen-over slog on a good wicket, or came in at 20 for 3 on a bad track. In neither case was that good training for a young player, and certainly no use for a Test career. Ken Barrington tells me that the great batsmen of his era would struggle in the limited-

176

HELMETS

Dennis Amiss was the man mainly responsible for popularizing the use of the helmet in first-class cricket in 1978. Dennis had been vulnerable against pace and the short-pitched ball for several seasons beforehand, and when he signed for World Series Cricket he realized that he would need protective headgear to combat the buffeting he knew he would receive from Lillee and all the others. Many old-timers scoffed at him, but a few modern cricketers who played the game for a living were convinced that a fatality was not far away. I was one of them; in fact I had advocated headgear for some time. Anyway, Dennis started off with the two crash helmet designs, moved on to the one with the grille, and then in 1979 he marketed the two he's holding. They are light, reasonably comfortable, and – whatever the purists say – they are here to stay. It is because the seventies was the decade of speed that the helmets were needed. But the helmet has lead to an abuse by close-in fielders; I do not see why they should be allowed to wear one, because it allows them to get even nearer to the batsman and so gives them an unfair advantage.

over game, because it was reduced to a formula where the fielding side was in control of things. The quality of fielding was so good, the field placings so defensive, and the bowling so negative that it was hard work to get on top. Apart from the third innings of a championship match, the English county cricketer played nothing but limited-overs cricket between 1974 and 1980. In the old days, great players such as May, Cowdrey, and Graveney learned their trade in an unhurried playing atmosphere; they also got plenty of chances to play long innings, with thirty-two championship matches being played.

I believe we should scrap the three-day championship match and play sixteen games of four-day duration. Those games would be played in the week, with a day to spare for travelling; and at the weekend we could have two days of limited-over cricket. The weekend stuff would get money in the bank, because many prefer the instant brand of cricket, while the traditionalists would still have their specialized stuff in midweek. If the midweek games get enough sponsorship, there could be two sorts of cricket: the midweek kind for the members and the players, and the weekend brand for the general public who want to see a finish inside a few hours.

If one accepts that Test cricket is still the summit of the game, then we should do all we can to improve England's standing in that area – and cutting back on overseas players would help. Not before time, their numbers are being reduced, but in the last decade we have suffered at the hands of countries who have had their best players trained in English cricket. Now we have a system where some cynical counties may be exploiting a loophole to keep a star overseas player in the side, while playing another overseas cricketer. Mike Procter and Brian Davison are no more English than Dame Edna Everage, but they are eligible for England, because they have played over here long enough without representing their countries in Test cricket. Their counties were quick to realize that, with restrictions on overseas players imminent, they had to do something – so Procter and Davison are now English. I cannot see how buying a house in England is a sufficient qualification for playing for England, and this whole charade only confirms how important winning has become to both players and officials. In this respect, I can appreciate Yorkshire's attitude: they have looked at the wider implications and stuck to their guns about only men born in the county playing for them. In my view, a British passport should be the main qualification for England eligibility, not successful bending of the rules.

Not until the 1981 season did we introduce covered wickets in English county cricket. I have never understood why the pitch should be left open to the vagaries of the weather until play is called off for the day. With wickets covered and the game longer, the captains will have to think about actually bowling a side out, rather than containing them for a certain number of overs. On good wickets, a medium-pace trundler cannot get class batsmen out – the successful bowler must be able to beat the bat with skill. If you have to stay out in the field because the game lasts longer, you will then look for bowlers of ability, rather than the boring diet of seam.

The game lacks variety in England, as in most other countries, and it is doing our Test prospects no good at all. The hundred-over limitation was introduced in 1974, since when the standard of our Test batting has gone down dramatically. If our performances in Tests improved, I believe more people would go and watch the national side in this country. The public would love to see us thrash the Aussies and the West Indies.

One of the biggest problems in world cricket in the eighties is going to be the standard of umpiring. I believe it is getting worse all over the world – including England, where we rightly pride ourselves on having the best. All the money that is flying around now has taken away most of the sportsmanship I knew when I first came into the game. Almost nobody walks now: when I saw Nigel Popplewell of Somerset walk in a championship match last season against Warwickshire, it hit me that I had not seen someone do that for a long time. I think the overseas players' influence in this respect has been bad – many of them just stand there, even for a caught and bowled. Tony Greig's example in the England side affected many others and, as a result, there are few players left who actually try to help the umpire. The umpire has to be in charge, and his performance can make or break a match; but now there is too much pressure on him. He cannot rely on somebody walking off if he has nicked it or only appealing if he thinks the batsman is out. I appeal a lot more now – when you see your batsmen given out on every third or fourth L.B.W. appeal, you simply have to do the same to stay in the contest. It is only in the last few years that English umpires have been getting decent money: to be a skilful umpire is as difficult as being a skilful player, and it takes character and nerve to stick the finger up at the right time.

I wonder how men like Charlie Elliott or Sid Buller would have reacted to the new breed of histrionic appealers and non-walking

179

DEFENSIVE FIELD PLACING

Before changes in the rules for the 1981 season this was a typical field that faced the frustrated batsman in the last few overs of a county championship innings. Because of the hundred-over limit on the first innings of a county match, the emphasis from the fielding captain was invariably placed on defence, as soon as the shine was off the ball on a good wicket. Getting the batsman out became less important than stopping him getting hold of the bowlers; fielders were taken away from catching positions and deployed in run-saving positions. A 'sweeper' fielder was used on either side about twenty yards from the bat and, even if the batsman got the ball past them, there were always men on the boundary to cut off the possible four. The result was stalemate, and field placing that looked just like something from the Sunday League. Now that the overs limitation has been scrapped, such defensive field placings as this will go out of fashion. Bowlers will have to get batsmen out.

batsmen. I fancy Dennis Lillee would have cut down on tantrums overseas with umpires of that strength of character around.

It has been suggested in many quarters that the answer to the poor umpiring in Tests abroad is to have an international panel of umpires and to fly them in for a series, in the way that soccer referees are used for internationals. The idea sounds good in theory, but what would they do between the Tests? Coach umpires? I would like to know how you coach an umpire – it is not like batting or bowling, where you can see the end product in the nets. You would need some very sophisticated video equipment to be able to monitor an umpire during a day's play and then show him where he went wrong. Everything is down to the split second in an umpire's job, and the margin between right and wrong is tiny. Take one example: the bat/pad catches that have everyone jumping around shouting, 'Catch it!' whenever the ball is in the air. They are the most difficult ones to judge, and you will always get a few wrong: in India with Tony Greig's team, our fielders close in on the leg-side would swear on their mothers' lives that the batsman had nicked the ball, while those on the off-side had not heard a thing. I have heard Tony laugh at the fact that the Indians did not appeal enough when he was offering bat/pad catches. One of their short legs would gather the ball, without realizing that Greig had nicked it onto his pad. Greig would not walk; but it just shows the difficulty facing an umpire. He is supposed to adjudicate from twenty yards away when the fielders a couple of feet from the bat are undecided.

That kind of skilful assessment under pressure cannot come from coaching; it must come from playing the game regularly. You do not need to have been a top player, but as long as you know the ins and outs of the game, you have got a chance. Knowledge of the laws is not enough, I am afraid.

Over rates are going to be a vexed issue until something positive is done. It is nonsense that England get fined for not reaching the required rate, while other countries get away with it. The West Indies' excuse that people come to see them, so therefore the public are not being cheated, is just hogwash; they bowl their overs slowly because it suits them tactically. Why should they bowl fewer balls an hour than the opposition and have the cheek to say they are entertaining the crowd? They say fines for slow over rates make the game artificial, but I believe 13 overs an hour is artificial – they *must* be able to bowl quicker, and the I.C.C. must introduce a rate of about 96 balls an hour. Otherwise, the West Indies will continue to have an unfair advantage.

I wish something could be done about the wickets. They have got slower all round the world – something I cannot understand, because surely perfect climatic conditions should produce fast wickets? There is some excuse in rainy countries like England and New Zealand. In Australia, however (although I do not really understand the nature of groundsmanship), I cannot see any good reason for their wickets having changed from being absolute belters in 1970–1 to green, underprepared ones in 1974–5, and then slow, low ones at present.

The groundsman who impressed me most in England was Gordon Prosser, who turned out the best wicket in the country at Worcester in the mid-seventies. He would be out early in the morning in mid-February, and would cross-roll the square till late at night. He would roll and roll it until the start of the season, and the result was a good, fast wicket with something in it for bowlers and batters. He drifted out of the game for a time and I am delighted he is back in county cricket with Somerset.

I would like to see England have a full-time salaried team manager for Test cricket. Alec Bedser has laboured long and hard, and perhaps he has done as much as one man can. A team boss with a selection committee should have the power to coach as well as judge a player. The best critics can get terribly one-eyed about a man. They can go to Northampton, where the ball seldom bounces nine inches, and see Wayne Larkins and Peter Willey look masterful players, but will they be able to bat like that in a Test? Selecting a side is a very difficult job – and it is not as if you are picking from all that many players in the first place. In the last five years the only England opening bowlers to choose from were Hendrick, Old, Botham, Lever and myself, while they picked the batsmen from a hard core of about twelve. The overseas players cornered the market too often. What I would like to see is a return to the idea of sending England Under-Twenty-five teams abroad. Now things like the Whitbread scholarships to Australia are very useful for three or four young lads a year; but there is no substitute for being part of a team on tour, trying to adapt to the conditions and helping each other out. The last England Under-Twenty-five team to leave these shores went to Pakistan in 1966–7, under the captaincy of Mike Brearley – and ten of that party have played for the full England side.

At last more imagination is being shown by the T.C.C.B. in assessing the registration rules for English county cricketers. A decade ago, there were no such things as industrial tribunals and applications to High Court judges for injunctions; you were put out to graze for a period of time, and you just accepted it if you felt strongly enough to want to move from one county to another. I suffered from that attitude, because Lord's thought I had put myself on the open market when I decided to leave Surrey. That was not true – the *counties* approached me – but I was still banned until 1 July before I could make my Warwickshire début in 1972. Nowadays you cannot stop a guy from moving to another county, because that would be tantamount to preventing him from earning a living. I think a compensation scheme should be introduced, whereby the club that nurtured the departing player's talent would get a certain amount of cash. It is generally accepted that it takes about five years to turn an English-born cricketer into a county player, so it seems a shame

183

SPONSORSHIP

The shape of things to come in cricket: the England team are getting more and more involved in endorsing such products as table cricket games (Botham and me) and coffee (Lever, Gower, Edmonds, and Gooch). Cornhill Insurance feature prominently on the tee-shirts – and deservedly so when you consider how much they have done for Test Cricket in England since 1977. In fact, the amount they paid to an England player for appearing in a Test is now totally out of proportion. I thought £1,000 a fair enough sum in 1977; but it is linked to the cost of living, and it has gone up by another £400 within three years. I am glad that the £1,400 fee has been frozen for the 1981 season. Anything above the £1,000 mark should be handed over to the counties, because the bread-and-butter players should get a sight of this cash. After all, some of them could be in the Test team anyway, and England players are earning more than enough money. The seventies may be remembered as the decade when the lawyers made stacks of cash out of cricket, but just as much was made by the agents of the top players.

that a county loses its investment in someone when he ups and leaves as soon as he has established himself. So I think the county that signs the player from another side should pay some sort of transfer fee, assessed on the work done to get the player up to standard.

I think the days of the benefit are numbered in England. It is a fundamentally semi-feudal system that causes embarrassment to the player and often results in a serious loss of form that becomes permanent. In the old days, the benefit was the carrot that kept a bloke at a county when he was tempted to go elsewhere. Club officials are kinder today, but I still believe that if we were paid higher wages, we would not need a benefit. If county membership fees went up, we would be paid more and there would be no need to pass the begging-bowl around later on. Membership subscriptions are remarkably good value in these inflationary days, especially for Test grounds like Trent Bridge, Edgbaston and Lord's. It has got like the TV licence fee: people take it for granted and moan about it when it gets increased, while forgetting about the great value one gets from BBC. Anyone who travels abroad a fair amount will confirm how lucky British TV viewers are, and the same applies to our county members.

Television has been a major instrument in getting cricket across to the public – indeed the biggest split the game has ever known originated in a TV squabble between Kerry Packer and the Australian

185

Board. It remains to be seen if TV sells cricket short: a whole generation of cricket fans may be growing up who prefer watching the TV highlights with all the tedious bits taken out and no need to sit on a hard seat at the ground. There is no doubt you get a better view from the armchair. I think the Australian idea of limiting coverage of home Tests is a good one: if a current Test is staged at Melbourne, there is coast-to-coast live coverage apart from the state of Victoria. There, it is only available after four o'clock, so viewers could only see the last two hours. The idea behind that is to try to get as many people in and around the Melbourne area to come along to the ground. The same system is applied for Perth, Sydney, Brisbane and Adelaide. It could be done in England: the BBC has its own regional programmes when it opts out of the network coverage, and things could be arranged so that viewers in the BBC Midland area, for example, would only get the last two hours of the Trent Bridge or the Edgbaston Test.

Although the BBC's coverage of Test cricket has been excellent over the years, I can visualize them losing exclusive rights pretty soon. Money is the name of the game, and the BBC is short of that. The T.C.C.B. has developed a keener awareness of financial matters, and will be watching the establishment of the second commercial channel with great interest. I would not be at all surprised if ITV–2 eventually makes the T.C.C.B. an offer it just cannot refuse – after all, if there is a lot of money available, the T.C.C.B. has a duty to plough that back into the game if all other conditions are met.

Financial considerations have become more and more important, but I suppose that is a symptom of our society, rather than of cricket itself. Just as politics cannot be divorced from sport, so sport is a mirror of the times in which we live. That is why many young cricketers do not work hard enough, why behaviour on the field has got worse, why there is so much sharp practice around in the game – it is part of life, and life in the seventies may have been exciting, but it was also materialistic and opportunist.

I have many wishes for cricket in the future, and if only some of them come true, the game will be even healthier than it is now. In England, I would want our batting to improve, to discover a crop of reliable, fit fast bowlers so that Willis & Co. can be put out to graze at last, and to watch our national team recover the self-respect we had in the fifties when Peter May had such a great side. There is too much of a feeling that it is good for cricket if we lose to India or New Zealand or someone else; no other country thinks in such public-school terms, so why not concentrate on becoming a great side again, instead of indulging in patronizing rhetoric? Now that the county championship has been restructured, we should be able to see whether England's decline is only temporary. I am convinced the 1974–80 set-up was harmful to our Test prospects, and I only know a few county cricketers who do not want to see four-day championship games on covered wickets. Some of the travelling should be cut down from an English season; the overseas players cannot believe we play so much, and by mid-season they are whacked.

As much emphasis should be placed on practising skills as on getting fit. I believe we have gone a little too far towards turning cricketers into athletes, rather than skilful performers who are also fit. I would hate to see us go the same way as English soccer, where the players often do not see a ball in training. There is no point in being fit enough to bowl long spells if you spray the ball all over the place and can't bowl where your captain wants. That comes with practice and dedication.

Abroad, I would like to see an improvement in the umpiring, by giving umpires more money, and thereby encouraging ex-players back to the game. So much stems from strong umpiring: unruly players will knuckle down to a disciplinarian and just get on with it.

In Australia, I would like to see some recognition from their Board that Test cricket is still vital, and that their flirtation with one-day cricket is only a temporary, money-making fad. Their crowds should be more tolerant and fairer to the opposition, although that is tantamount to asking for a national change in character. Less gamesmanship and more guys like Kim Hughes, Jeff Thomson and Rodney Hogg would also be a nice thought.

For South Africa, I wish a return to Test cricket and a continuation of their policy of playing only one overseas man per team in first-class cricket. Here they have got their priorities right where the English counties have not.

It would be nice to see the West Indians bowl their overs quicker, an end to treating their spinners like lepers, and bigger grounds, so that more people will come and watch, and their superb players will then deservedly get more money and better facilities.

I hope the Indian players stay as sporting as Viswanath in the Jubilee Test, and that they do not get carried away with one-day cricket after their Australian tour. The pace of life in India is ideally suited to Test cricket, and I trust the success of Kapil Dev will not stop the flow of great spin bowlers from that country.

187

From Pakistan, there is a need for a more positive attitude from their captains, and a realization that defeat will not mean that the side are publicly executed by order of the Government. I hope their succession of great batsmen does not end with this present crop, and that their wickets improve. Those slow, low ones could hardly get worse.

In New Zealand, it would be nice to see cricket break rugby's stranglehold. Their Cricket Board is so short of cash that they have to beg visiting countries to give up their rest day if rain has washed out much play in a Test match. Otherwise the crowds would be even smaller, and they would be further in debt. I hope they remain as hospitable in New Zealand as they have been in the past, and that not too many teams come to them at the fag-end of an exhausting tour elsewhere. More coaches from English counties will help eliminate that amateur image; and it would be nice to see Glenn Turner forget his differences with the Establishment and prove that he can match Sunil Gavaskar century for century.

Some of these are pipe-dreams, of course. I suspect that the game will get even harsher, and I hope its hold on the public's affection is not going to be slackened still further as we move into an age where the working man will get even greater leisure time. Cricket has moved enough with the modern times in my opinion, and I believe it is time it re-asserted many of its traditional virtues. I hope the eighties do not hold as many harmful changes for cricket as did the previous decade. Many of us have made a good living from cricket, and I trust we will be on hand to help it when our playing days are done.

It may be that by the end of the 'eighties, Test cricket as I know it will have changed radically. The Robin Jackman Affair of 1981 signified that politics and sport are solidly intertwined, and that financial considerations complicate the issue even further. I believe the Cricket Council was right to threaten to call off the England tour to the West Indies in the face of political pressure from Guyana. In the end, the need for a profit from England's tour was the crucial factor for the West Indies cricket administrators and politicians. However, it would be very naïve to assume that politics will not enter the Test arena again in the next few years and perhaps cause a break-up of the existing order.

PHOTO
ACKNOWLEDGEMENTS

The authors and publishers would like to thank the following for the use of their photographs: *The Cape Argus*, p. 104; Patrick Eagar, pp. 12, 16, 18, 23, 25, 36, 39 (left and right), 42, 44, 49, 56, 57, 58, 61, 67, 70, 71, 80, 89, 107, 109, 119, 120–1, 129, 133, 138, 143, 144, 148, 150, 153, 160, 164, 172, 174; Ken Kelly, pp. 11, 20-21, 27, 29, 31, 32, 93, 95, 99, 113, 116, 122, 126, 136 (left and right), 146, 155, 162, 167, 177, 180–1, 184, 185; The Press Association Ltd, pp. 73, 103; *The Sun*, p. 53.

INDEX